Tucks

Textures

& Pleats

by

Jennie Rayment

Acknowledgements

This book is dedicated to all my friends, family and Rene - without their mutual support and help, none of this would have ever happened.

Specifically my heartfelt thanks are extended to Basil Crisp and Nick Diment for their unflagging help in proof reading and correcting all the horrendous mistakes; Geoff Mullery for his kindness in converting the Word Processor discs; Shelagh Jarvis for all her help in making samples and the beautiful quilt in addition to her friendly support; Sue Wood, Anne Smith and Lesley Seddon for the loan of their work for the photographs; Margot Abrahams and Angie McKimm for their splendid ideas; and Elizabeth Cobbett for the loan of her photocopier.

Also, a big thank you to John Plimmer, the photographer, and Derry Morgan, the printer, without whose help and advice this book would not be so good.

Finally, I thank all the students who have suffered from my teaching and still returned for more! Without the inspiration of teaching and meeting so many delightful people, my life would have been very empty.

Copyright © Jennie Rayment 1994
First Published November 1994
Revised and Reprinted March 1996
by J. R. Publications
Wren Cottage,
3 The Millstream,
Haslemere, Surrey GU27 3QA.
01428 652495

ISBN 0-9524675-4-2

Photography by Jaypics
10 The Pallant,
Havant, Hampshire PO9 1BE.
01705 476624/470310

Printed by St. Richard's Press Limited
Leigh Road, Terminus Industrial Estate,
Chichester, West Sussex PO19 2TU.
01243 782988

Tiles and Pottery kindly loaned for the photographs by Zydeco 01705 469119

Contents

Introduction

Tantalise with Tucks.
Beguile with the Bias.
Enter the fascinating world of textural creativity!

Be guided through the tactile delights of fabric manipulation. Discover the simplicity and explore the diversity, as you create a unique masterpiece.

**It's easy, it's fun and it's different,
and making mistakes will not matter!**

I have been teaching these methods for a number of years, and there is nothing nicer than being able to reassure new students -

"Every one can make all these exciting and innovative textural creations. The ability to sew a straight line is not really necessary - it's helpful, but the end product may be better, certainly different, with a few added minor deviations. After all, variety is the spice of life!"

Very little equipment is required. The samples can be stitched by hand or by machine. The basic model will cope with all the techniques. An accurate seam allowance is not always essential, the designs can be planned as you sew, changes can be made and only you will know if the final result is perhaps not quite the original idea!

**'Experience is the name everyone gives to their mistakes'
(Oscar Wilde 1892)**

****

Have confidence and give it a go!

*Gather up the fabric,
collect your equipment,
clear a space on the table,
frozen t.v. dinner tonight, and let's begin!*

Equipment and Fabrics

The basic essentials that most students will find most useful (in addition to the usual sewing accessories) are -
1. Rotary cutter
2. Rotary ruler
3. Cutting mat
4. Hand or Electric sewing machine.

A machine is not necessary as all the techniques may be done by hand, but it does speed up the process.

Rotary Cutters

There are many different cutters on the market, ranging from the *Olfa, Dritz* and *Kai. (See List of Stockists.)*

The larger size of the *Olfa* cutter is the one I prefer; it is comfortable to hold, cuts through many layers at once and I find it more controllable than the smaller one. In addition, the *Olfa* cutter can be screwed up tightly, so small children cannot experiment on the furniture with this lovely yellow gadget that cuts nice thin lines.

When buying an *Olfa* rotary cutter for the first time, do remember to slacken the screw on the back, something the instructions do not mention. Omitting this prevents the blade from rotating correctly; after some time the screw becomes loose and the blade will only partially cut the fabric, due to the over-use of one section of the wheel.

Begin by slightly loosening the screw on the back and when you have finished cutting out, tighten again, rendering the cutter less accessible for those little fingers to experiment with. In addition, this prevents the guard sliding open when the cutter is in the bottom of the bag.

DO NOT FORGET TO REPLACE THE GUARD IMMEDIATELY YOU HAVE MADE ANY CUT.

Too many accidents are caused by open blades.

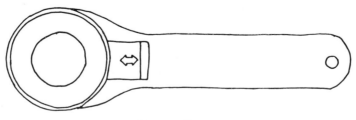

Rotary Cutter

Dritz and *Kai* cutters are extremely useful for arthritic or less flexible hands, as no force is required to release the guard: it automatically retracts when you apply pressure. Consequently when the cutter is pushed along any surface, it will score beautifully!

Using the Cutter

Some people have difficulty cutting with this tool. A few problems that occur are –

1. Failure to cut the beginning/end of the fabric.

Start cutting slightly before the beginning of the material and run the cutter off the end of the cloth.

2. Failure to cut through all the layers.

Apply firmer pressure, the blade will not damage the board. Push the cutter away from you – easier than pulling it towards the body and safer if you slip.

3. Failure to cut straight lines.

Ensure the blade is next to the ruler, the guard on the outside away from the ruler. Check the material is folded flat with no creases. Try ironing the fabric before cutting.

Rotary cutting Mats

There are many different mats on the market. Some are "self-healing" – the surface cannot be damaged with cutting, providing the blade is intact. Small slivers could be removed from the surface of the board if you 'saw' through any uncut portion of fabric. The non-self-healing mats will damage with use, but are less expensive.

When purchasing a mat, there are several different sizes. The smaller ones are ideal for carrying to classes, but the available surface area is not so useful for cutting large strips. The medium size [17″ (43cm) x 23″ (60cm)] is preferable.

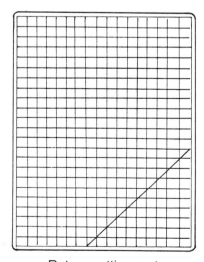
Rotary cutting mat

Some mats have grid and angle lines superimposed; these are helpful for lining up the material, but not totally necessary if you possess a Rotary Cutting Ruler, (see below).

Whichever mat you finally select, keep it flat at all times, and <u>please</u> do not leave it in the sun as the excessive heat will warp the surface. It appears that nothing will remove those wrinkles and you can't give it a face lift!

Rotary Cutting Rulers

Once again, as there is a tremendous choice and variety on the market, you can quickly be bamboozled into purchasing more rulers than you need.

I would recommend starting with the large *"Quilter's Rule"* 6½" (16cm) x 24" (60cm). Most of the cutting tasks can be performed with this ruler; the print is clear and the ridged back will grip the material and prevent it slipping. The only drawback may be the overall length and you may prefer the shorter length – 14" (35cm) x 4½" (12cm). As with all things, everyone has a personal preference, and what is suitable for one may not be for someone else!

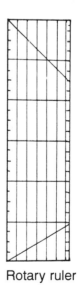

Do check that the selected rotary cutting ruler measures accurately. As the printed lines are fairly thick, it is important to discover which part of the line relates to the accurate measurement. Test the spacings with another ruler. For Tucks and Textures; there is no need for absolute accuracy, often a straight cut is all that is required.

Rotary ruler

Measuring with the Rotary Ruler

Confusion can strike when you are first faced with all these new gadgets. All you wish to do is is to cut a strip off the cloth. Easy really!!

Try this method.

1. Press the fabric first. Fold, lining up the selvedges, re-fold into four, matching the fold to the selvedge (fig. 1).

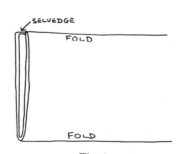

SELVEDGE
FOLD
FOLD

Fig 1

2. Before cutting any width, trim the beginning of the cloth (it may be unevenly cut). Position the ruler completely on top of the fabric; check that the folds are parallel with the lines on the ruler and the mat; slide the ruler to the raw edge; place your hand firmly on the ruler and slice the edge straight with the cutter (fig. 2).

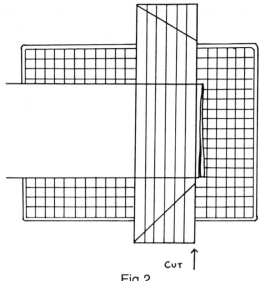

CUT

Fig 2

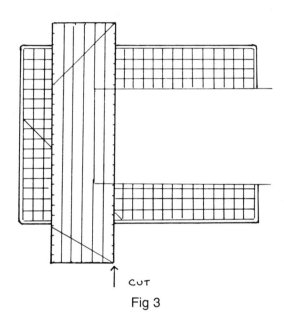

CUT

Fig 3

3. Place the fabric on the right side of the cutting mat, the ruler on the left. Slide the ruler on to the fabric until the desired measurement is reached, i.e. the ruler covers the required amount of fabric to be cut.

*Fab **R** ic on the right*
*Ru **L** er on the left.*

(Left handed students reverse the directions)

4. Hold the ruler steady with your hand and push the cutter blade away from you up the side of the ruler (fig.3).

Sewing Machines

All the techniques can be created without a machine; it just takes a little longer!

There is no need for anything more advanced than a basic hand or electric model. Hopefully, you will be able to sew a straight line with a medium stitch length - 10 stitches/inch (4 stitches/cm). The straight stitch presser foot is ideal for most of the techniques; a zipper foot would be useful for fine tucks, piping and inserting zips. Pin Tucks do need a special presser foot - see section on Zipper Foot Tucks and Pin Tucks.

If you do possess a sewing machine, keeping it lightly oiled and free from fluff will prolong its life, cut down on servicing costs and improve the performance. My machines have a lot of use, so they are cleaned and oiled most weeks, but if you do not use the machine a tremendous amount, it need not be attended to as frequently, i.e. a little more than once in a blue moon!! A routine maintenance at the end of a long project is ideal; clean the dust out, oil the moving parts, but -

OIL ONLY WHERE IT IS RECOMMENDED
IN THE INSTRUCTION BOOK

Running the machine fast afterwards will allow the fine oil to lubricate all the moving parts and it will be ready for the next project.

Use a medium size of needle (80) when you are sewing with medium weight calico; a finer needle (70) for lightweight fabrics; for applying frills, backs to cushions and/or heavy weight materials, it is advantageous to use a large needle (100). Needles should always be straight and sharp; they blunt with time and use, so do change them sometimes. Be careful that the tip is intact or it could snag the work and the machine will seem to be hammering or tapping more than normal.

Most threads are suitable for use in the machine, ranging from polyesters to mercerised cottons. Sewing machines appear to prefer the same type and make of thread on the top spool and in the bobbin. Although - *invisible thread should only be used on the top spool with a cotton or polyester thread underneath.*

Sometimes changing the threads can upset the tension on the machine. If the top thread is lying on the surface and not locked evenly into the lower thread, you have to slacken the tension on the top thread.

On the front of the machine, there is a dial, with either a (+) or (-), or a series of numbers from 1 to 10; normally the indicator line will be approximately in the centre of the dial, but to slacken the top tension, turn the dial to the (-) or a lower number. This allows the top thread to run more freely, interlocking with the lower thread in a uniform manner. Should the reverse situation be apparent, with lower thread lying tautly and not locked correctly into the top thread, the tension dial should be turned to a higher number or towards the (+).

Some makes of machine have a sewing table attachment; this is useful for supporting the work and provides a space for the left hand while guiding the material.

Finding The Seam Allowance on the Machine

Trying to sew accurate seam allowances can be a great problem although a little variation does not matter with Tucks and Textures! To be able to run the edge of the presser foot down the fabric with the needle set a ¼" (.5cm) from the side of the foot is extremely helpful in sewing accurate quarter-inch or half centimetre seams.

Many of the older machines have a presser foot that is ¼" from the needle to the side of the foot. There is a special presser foot for many modern machines that is made for this seam allowance. Try asking your stockist for the correct presser foot.

Other machines have several needle positions and they can be set to produce ¼" (.5cm) from the needle to the side of the presser foot. The older Elna models can have the needle set slightly off centre: move the dial carefully until the needle is in the correct place, mark the front of the machine with a pencil; the needle will remain at this position providing you have moved it carefully.

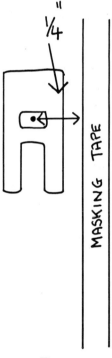

If there is no possible method of moving the needle, try sticking a piece of masking tape to the body of the sewing machine, setting it at the desired seam allowance from the needle. Machines that are supplied with a narrow hem foot only and machines with large presser feet will benefit from this trick (fig. 4).

Fig 4

As a last resort, you can rule the seam allowance on to the fabric using a hard sharp pencil and sew on the pencil line.

Treat yourself to a 'Quilter's Quarter'- a specially designed ¼" square ruler.

Choice of Fabrics

Calico

Calico is a plain woven cloth, sometimes bleached, mainly sold in Britain in the unbleached state. It is distinguished by the dark fleck of fibrous cotton that occurs intermittently. Sometimes loomstate calico has coloured threads caught in the weave; this is the basic raw material, prior to any refining process. The name calico originates from Calcutta Cloth, from the Indian city that initially exported it.

In America, calico is a printed cloth with a figured pattern, and the British calico is called muslin. This can cause confusion as muslin in England is a fine loose weave, certainly not suitable for Tucks and Textures.

Calico varies from supplier to supplier. You will find an assortment of different weights, weaves and colours. Use a medium weight cloth with a firm weave. The finer weaves do not support the pleats and folds that create the design. Thick weaves are too rigid to twist in the various patterns. Also some of the fabrics have fire resistant dressings; these are frequently too stiff for use in textured work.

A further advantage of calico is the cost. It is relatively inexpensive compared to other materials; consequently, you can use it with gay abandon and really explore all the exciting and innovative ideas found in this book.

Washing Calico

Most of of the samples that are shown in the photographs are made from unwashed calico. The fabric has not been washed as the manufacturers' dressings stiffen the material and it is easier to manipulate.

Your hands will go up in horror at this flagrant disobedience of all the rules, but if you wash the calico beforehand, it is difficult to remove the creases with the iron. The material needs to be pressed when damp; using a hot iron can singe the surface, so do be careful.

Placing the material after washing and damp drying in the deep-freeze for 30 minutes makes the pressing easier.

Calico cushions do need washing - in my house that is not often; after all who wants to spend time washing cushions when one can play with another technique?

To wash the cloth successfully - hand-wash in warm water, cool rinse, remove the excess water by rolling in a towel; tumble until almost dry and if essential, lightly press. If the article is a cushion, push the pillow/pad (feather or polyester) inside before tumbling on a medium heat, remove when almost dry, either "air" in the airing-cupboard or toss it on the sofa, and do not rest the weary head until it has dried properly! If a tumble-dryer is not part of the household equipment, still replace the pillow/pad as this keeps the shape while drying.

Other Types of Fabrics

Textured effects look equally interesting in other plain materials or small self-patterned prints. Use of chintz (glazed cotton) creates attractive areas of light and shadow due to the sheen on the cloth from the glazing. Chintz can become limp after washing, as the glaze washes off; apparently there are no products that restore the surface.

There is a wide choice of fabrics on the market from gabardines, light-weight denims, sateens, satins, silks, tickings and cretonnes. All of these can be used for textured samples. A simple tucked cushion will be totally different in another type of cloth.

To Rip or not to Rip

Having broken the rules concerning washing the fabric, tearing it is not a good idea. If you rip the material, the edge will be stretched and damaged. Tearing is only ideal for producing a frayed edge.

When cloth is ripped, it tears along the weft thread. A problem is caused if the weft thread is not straight (a frequent occurrence in the modern mechanical weaving process); the tear could then be a slanting line. We have all experienced trying to re-align the material - so be kind, cut the cloth, don't rip it!

Choice of Threads

As discussed in the section on machines, most threads can be used. Matching coloured thread will maximise the textural effect and disguise any mistakes. Contrasting threads will add a further feature to the design, but any deviation from the chosen path will show!

Thread Savers

A really neat idea for saving an enormous amount of thread was shown to me by one of my students.

"The Thread Saver" is simply a scrap of fabric that you sew on to after stitching any seam. The connecting threads between the last section and the Thread Saver are cut at the back of the presser foot (fig. 5).

Little thread is wasted with this method of continuous sewing. It ensures that the threads do not get consumed by the feed dogs or jam in the needle plate.

Another advantage of this natty notion occurs when you commence sewing on a thick material or begin stitching with the zipper foot; the material feeds more easily under the presser foot as it is already sitting on a fabric surface, i.e. the Thread Saver.

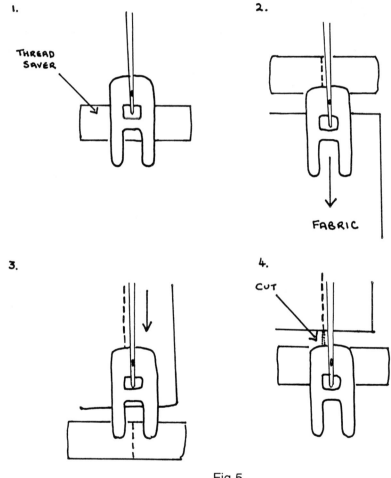

Fig 5

Sew on and off Thread Saver.
Cut threads from back of presser foot.

Tucks in Calico: featuring Trumpets in the corners (Jennie Rayment).

Stripey Tucks: Chintz cushion and fabric basket with a plaited handle made from padded strips (Jennie Rayment).

Origami Twist: with folded pleats and free machine quilting (Jennie Rayment).

Lifted Star: Calico Star has Ruched Piping. Coloured Star features two coloured frill (Jennie Rayment).

Woven Calico Handbag and Bias Tuck Calico Belt: (Jennie Rayment).

Tucks and Pleats

Inspiration from natural to man-made design sources abounds when you cast an eye around. Any series of parallel lines or ridges can be used as a basis for the initial tucked effect.

Nature is brimming with ideas for tucks. The underside of mushrooms, the crags in rocks, ploughed lines in fields, bark of trees; some fruits and vegetables have ridged surfaces that could be translated into tucks. Landscapes and seascapes lend themselves to distorted and curvacious tuck formations. Have you ever seen straight waves?

Investigate your environment. Look at roof structures, staircases, scaffolding, tiles, aerial photographs, roads, railway tracks, bridges. Contemporary art and sculpture can display a linear format that may be expanded.

We are surrounded by lines in different patterns and arrangements which would all make starting points for your design. Then you can alter the patterns by flexing the tucks in different directions.

From art to architecture, sea to sky, ancient and modern, there is a wealth of creativity from the harmonious to the abstract.

Remember the golden rule -

MISTAKES DO NOT MATTER
THE RESULT IS JUST DIFFERENT

****

The most appealing part of making Tucks is choice. You can choose to have lots of tucks, very few tucks, thick ones, thin ones, wide spacings, narrow spacings, thick and thin tucks mixed in a sequence or at random and if you wish, deliberately regular or accidentally irregular tucks (only you will know which they are). The variety is tremendous. Until now you have probably always had to follow the designated seam allowances and persuade the pieces to fit, but now you are free to choose.

As all this choice can be unsettling, I have suggested certain spacings and seam allowances, so you will gain the confidence to play and discover new ideas for yourself.

How to Start The Tucks

As tucks take up space on the width of the fabric, to form a square it is advisable to cut an oblong (rectangle) from the calico. Tucks will lie more easily if you sew down the straight grain of the material (parallel to the selvedges) rather than across it. Matching thread (calico coloured) in the machine disguises unintentional mistakes.

1. Cut piece of calico approximately 24" (60cm) wide x 11" (28cm) deep.

Depth being down the selvedge.

2. Mark 1" (2.5cm) spacings with a pencil along both long edges (fig. 6).

Unnecessary to rule lines down the fabric as the pencil marks cannot be easily removed.

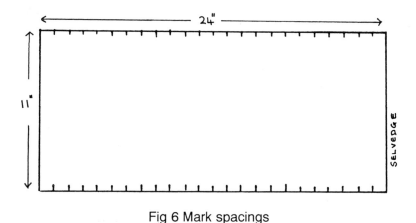

Fig 6 Mark spacings

3. Thread up the machine with matching thread on the top and bottom spool, and start stitching. Fold the fabric on the first set of marks, then sew down (fig. 7).

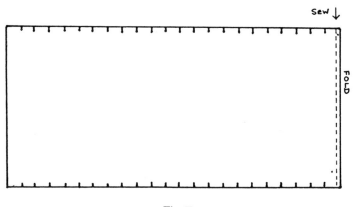

Fig 7

If you can run the edge of the presser foot down the fold, this will help to keep the tuck accurate. Some machines have several needle settings, and you can re-position the needle nearer to or further from the edge of the presser foot, making the tuck wider or narrower. Life should be easy and not like hard work - use the edge of the presser foot and keep it on the fold. Aim for approximately ¼" (.5cm) seam allowance.

Remember to use a Thread Saver! At the end of each line of stitching sew on to the saver, cutting the threads off at the back of the presser foot, (see Equipment section page 14).

4. Fold and sew down on every set of pencil marks (fig. 8). Do not start or finish the tucks too close to the side edges; leave space for a seam allowance for adding any borders.

Try to sew up one way and down the other; if the sewing is only done from one direction, the sample will distort.

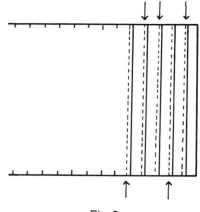
Fig 8
Change direction of sewing

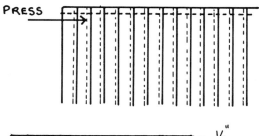

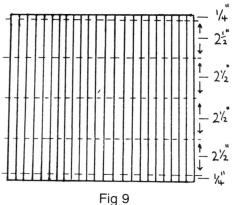
Fig 9

5. Press all the tucks in one direction. Stitch along the top side securing all the pleats; use quarter-inch seam allowance. Using a pencil or a marking pen, measure even spacings down the work (fig. 9).

These measurements could be equal e.g. 2 ½" (6cm) - or choose your own.

6. Sew along these lines flexing the tucks in different directions (sharp points of small scissors will help to hold them flat). Finally sew along the lower edge to stabilise the pleats (fig. 10).

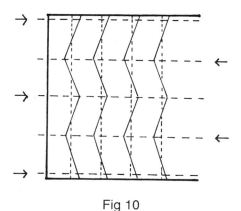
Fig 10

Developing the Theme

Try sewing diagonally across the work, or flexing the tucks in pairs, pushing two towards each other on one line, then alternate the effect on the next row of stitching (fig. 11).

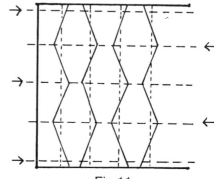

This makes a lovely honeycomb pattern, and depending on the initial depth of tucks sewn, fascinating areas of light and shadow appear. You can sew curved lines across representing a wave design, or to disguise a mistake. You do not have to sew straight - we know the wiggles were intended!

Fig 11

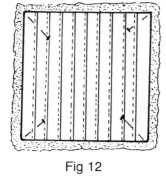

Fig 12

Placing the original tucked fabric on to wadding/batting before you perform the flexing will remove some of the buckling of the material. This will also quilt the work and anchor the surface. Pin the piece to the wadding/batting in each corner before starting (fig. 12).

Change the spacings as you flex the tucks - thick tucks will distort if the spacing is too close (fig. 13).

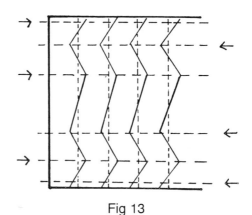

Fig 13

Circles can be most effective.

Cut a large circle of material and mark the centre. Set the point of a compass on this dot and draw a smaller circle. Line up the midpoint of a protractor with the centre and measure an equal series of degrees. Using a ruler draw a corresponding mark on the inner and outer circles
(fig. 14).

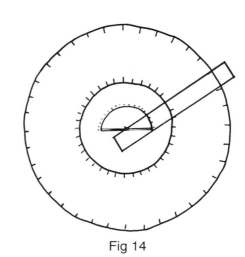

Fig 14

Cut out the inner circle - this will now resemble a giant Polo! Fold the fabric on the marks and sew the pleats, using the same seam allowance (fig. 15). Remember to alternate the direction of the stitching, (see colour photographs).

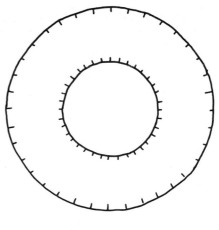

Cut out centre

As the sample is reduced in size because of the tucks, the circumference of the circles must measure more than the amount of fabric contained in the pleats. The circular wall-hanging shown in the coloured photographs was a 30" (75cm) diameter outer circle - 10" (25cm) diameter inner circle marked at 9° intervals (40 pencil marks) and with ¼" (.5cm) seams for the tucks.

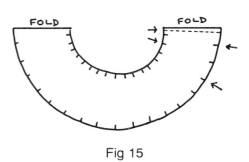

Fig 15

Extend the ideas into a panel, positioning sections with tucks flexed in different ways. Use the design for a headboard, wall-hanging, section of a quilt, part of a jacket or waistcoat. This technique is most effective for an impressive tie-back or cushions in abundance.

Deliberately sew random tucks with distorted folds to create the bark on trees or a geological formation. Quilt on to wadding/batting for additional texture.

Experiment with striped fabrics, sewing down or across the stripes. Really easy - the stripes will keep the sewing straight!

You can really do anything, the result is stunning.

"Give it a whirl and have a play!"

Zipper Foot Tucks
and Pin Tucks

Zipper Foot Tucks

You have seen how easy it is to use the normal presser foot to create wide pleats. Now try using the zipper foot to produce narrow tucks similar to pin tucks.

Glancing around, your immediate surroundings contain many objects with fine lines that would make an excellent design source for a series of zipper foot tucks, e.g. stripes in tartan fabrics and wallpapers; ridges in stone and pottery; rocky cracks, crags and crazy paving plus wrinkles of all description!

Why be creative when the world around us is teeming with ideas for us? Of course you could always conjure up a few of your own!

Creating a Zipper Foot Tuck

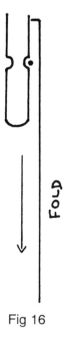

Put the zipper foot on the machine. Fold the fabric. Position the presser foot against the edge of the fabric fold (fig. 16).

Set the foot completely on the beginning of the material or the cloth can become chewed up in the feed dogs.

Fig 16

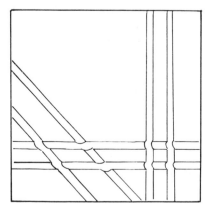

Fig 17

Sew along the fold in an orderly fashion (can't resist this phrase), re-fold the material and keep going. Explore the effect of the tucks in an organised format or an abstract fashion, possibly stitching tucks over tucks (fig. 17).

For hand sewing; use a small back-stitch or a close running stitch where the zipper foot stitching line would have been made.

Placing the tucked section on to wadding/batting with quilting between the tucks will add more emphasis to the texture. Random tucks make marvellous mountainous regions for a landscape. Reverse the work, the wrong side may be more interesting than the right side. Combine both aspects in the same sample - see landscape photograph also.

Zip Foot Tucks

Pin Tucks

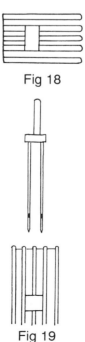

Fig 18

Fig 19

To produce pin tucks, a special presser foot is required (fig. 18), and it is rare for this to be standard issue with the sewing machine. In addition, a twin needle is used with two reels of thread.

Check when you purchase a pin tuck foot that you are sold the correct twin needle. The needles should fit between the grooves on the underside of the foot (fig. 19). There are several different types of pin tuck feet to choose from; the amount of grooves determines the size and spacing of the tucks.

Attach the foot to the machine and insert the twin needle. Check that the neck of the needle is correctly positioned (twin needles are expensive, and can snap easily if incorrectly placed). Thread up with the two spools of thread; on the top of the machine, there may be two spindles to hold the threads, but sometimes the threads need to be placed in tandem on the one spindle. On occasions, a carefully positioned knitting needle will suffice !

If your machine has a tension dial with a central metal ring, drop one thread either side of this ring; if not, place both threads through the normal channels. Try not to twist the threads before threading the needles. Ensure that the thread spools are of equal weight or the top tension can become unbalanced.

Finally tighten up the top thread tension, i.e. turn to a higher number or towards the (+) sign. This makes the pin tuck more pronounced.

Place the fabric completely underneath the presser foot. It is preferable to stitch quite slowly as the needles are fragile. Sewing down the diagonal/bias of the

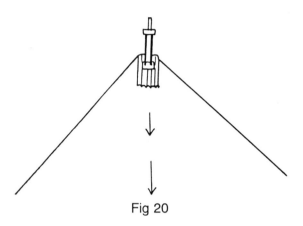

Fig 20

fabric has a marginally better effect than stitching down the straight grain (fig. 20).

Cord can be placed underneath the material, and the grooves of the foot will feed it through. It helps to hold the end of the cord as you start. Ensure that it remains in the centre of the foot or it can slip out and the cord will not be enclosed in the tuck. (Being of a lazy nature, I have to admit that I never use cord!)

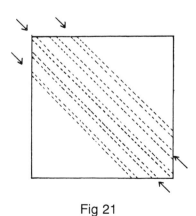

Fig 21

Now, sit there and get thoroughly bored with trundling up and down the fabric. Alternate the stitching directions or constantly sewing from the same edge will distort the material (fig. 21). Keeping the tucks straight is easy as one of the grooves in the foot can be aligned with the previous tuck. Just check that it remains in the same groove and the lines will be perfect!

Intriguing and fascinating patterns can be created using curved or random tucks or sections of straight tucks in different directions. Produce a large piece of pin tucked fabric, then cut up and use for patchwork.

Texturing in this fashion can be included in many types of garments. Inserting panels of pin tucks into cushions, quilts, head-boards and tie-backs will add an interesting touch. Use of different coloured threads in the machine will give even more variety.

But if you do not possess a pin tuck foot, twin needles can be used for decorative effect. These fine parallel lines in contrasting colours look delightful. You can even have zig-zag lines if you adjust the stitch width.

Do not adjust the width by more than half the maximum, or the needles will hit the presser foot and break.

Tuck in and explore all the possibilities!

Pin Tucked Amish Star

Crossing Over the Tucks

As in the previous chapters, a variety of different ways of tucking and pleating fabric has been developed; crossing tucks was mentioned in the pin tuck and zipper foot section.

One of my students, Angie Mckimm, was experimenting with a design, and discovered the exciting possibilities of tucking across previously constructed pleats.

This theme can be extended ad infinitum, and from her initial idea, I have extended it into a large panel. This is quick to produce, looks most attractive and has lots of avenues that could be explored.

Technically, it helps to be accurate with the measuring of the tucks, but who knows what exciting textural effects you may inadvertently discover?

****

Constructing a Crossed Tuck Panel

1. Cut a 24″ (60cm) square of calico. Mark equal divisions along the edges; suggest 8″ (20cm).

2. Fold on the diagonal, using 1¼″ (3cm) seam, sew across (fig. 22).

Take care not to stretch the material as it is on the bias.

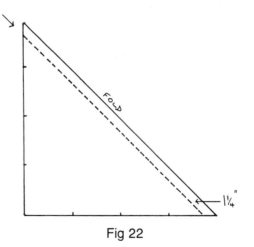

Fig 22

3. Repeat the tucking, on either side of the central pleat, using the same seam allowance as above. This gives 5 large tucks running across the calico (fig. 23).

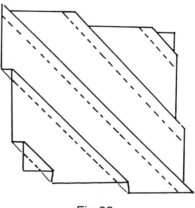

Fig 23

24

4. Press the tucks flat (fig. 24). (It will resemble box pleating.)

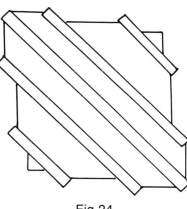

Fig 24

5. Repeat these tucks from the opposite sides using the same seam allowances, crossing over the flattened ones (fig. 25). Press these tucks flat in addition. The work should resemble a diagonal lattice approximately 15″ (38cm) square (see fig. 26).

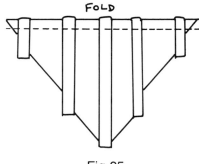

Fig 25

6. The panel will probably need to be squared up, as it may have distorted in the sewing. Carefully straighten the edges and it may be preferable to catch the central sections down to keep the crossed tucks stable.

Add borders for an interesting cushion or inset the panel into a quilt or as part of a head-board.

Extending the Technique

Now you have seen how easy it is to cross over tucks, try one tuck down the centre of a square, and one from the opposite side. Then experiment with this theme across a different shape, e.g. hexagon or octagon; Angie's original idea came from an octagonal shape. Investigate the effect of three tucks across a triangle, or six tucks across a hexagon, and so on.

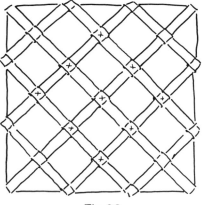

Fig 26

Secure the central crossing with a tassel, button, beads, French knots, bullion knots, pom-pom, cross-stitch or use a quilting tie of some description (fig. 26). Add more interest with contrasting coloured threads.

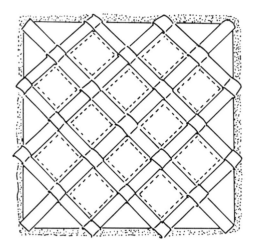

Fig 27

Place the completed panel on wadding and quilt in between the lattice work (fig. 27).

The edges of any tucks on the bias grain could be rolled.

Insert scraps of material under the folds.

Make the tucks straight across the original square forming a "noughts and crosses" design. Why not embroider 0 and X in the spaces?

Like so many of these textural ideas, the extensions are limitless - all you need is time !

Ruched and Gathered Textures

Not only can you tuck fabric but it can be gathered. Imagine the scrunched up effect of tiny pebbles, or the hide of an elderly elephant, or the nasty puckering of cellulite - cottage cheese bottoms!! Must not put you off as, in all honesty, ruched material has a most attractive appearance.

Using gathering techniques, you can achieve a smocked illusion; fine sections of gathering can be inserted to create a seer-sucker form of material; panels of "smocking" could be incorporated into fashion garments, cushions, tie-backs and pelmets - can you visualise the ruched and textured facade of a pelmet?

Ruched frills can be added to cushions, curtains, clothing and edges of small quilts. Different effects will be created by employing the bias or straight grain of the weave.

Ruched Inset

1. Cut a long strip of calico, or any other fabric. Select any width; suggest 2" (5cm); use the rotary cutter for accuracy. By either hand or using the longest stitch on the sewing machine, sew down one long edge (fig. 28).

Fig 28

If you tighten up the tension on the machine [higher number or towards the (+)], this will begin to gather the fabric for you. (Threads snapping or excessive gathering are caused by over-tightening the tension.)

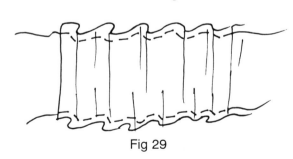

Fig 29

2. Repeat on the opposite edge, then draw up the threads; the top thread is already tighter due to the adjusted tension. Be careful not to pull so hard that the other end comes through! Continue gathering up until you have decided that the ruching is sufficient (fig. 29).

This strip can now be inserted into your work, with plain ungathered sections either side, if desired (fig. 30).

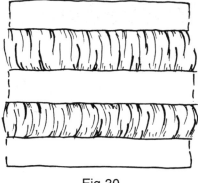

Fig 30

Several rows of gathering may be done or sets of closely spaced gathers can be secured by a wide satin stitch, in a contrasting thread colour. You could gather in a curved or undulating manner, depicting waves and the froth on the beach.

Ruched Frill

For a ruched frill, fold the gathered strip in half and stitch along the edge (fig. 31).

Add this for a different finishing method to cushions and curtains.

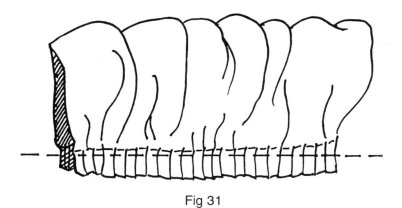

Fig 31

If the original strip was cut on the straight grain of the fabric, the appearance of the ruched frill will be slightly crisper than if you cut the strip from the bias, which has a more rounded effect.

Ruched Fabric

This looks absolutely stunning, but I must warn you that until you add a border to the sample, the result resembles that piece of prized work that you screwed up and discarded in disgust !

1. Cut a large square of the calico; ruching reduces the total area by four, i.e. 16"(40cm) square could end up only a 4" (10cm) piece. Set the machine for the long stitch as previously described; if your machine has a tacking facility this helps tremendously (use the smaller tacking length).

2. Follow the pattern shown in the diagram. Start in from the edge, sew across the calico, stop - do not break the thread. Turn the work and re-position the foot approximately ½"(1cm) away from the first line. Sew back to the beginning, now break the threads. Repeat this manoeuvre until you have covered all the fabric, then following the same technique stitch across the previously sewn lines (fig. 32).

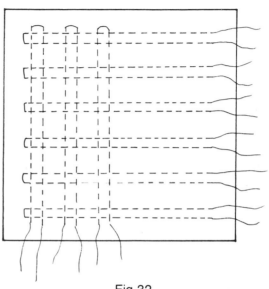

Fig 32

When I first tried this, I omitted to leave a space on the edge and consequently the top threads became confused with the underneath threads; this made it very hard to untangle which of the ends I should pull up. Also I failed to realise the value of sewing "U"s across the calico; hence when I pulled to gather, I pulled the entire thread through!

Fig 33

3. Now, holding the fabric firmly, pull up all the threads; be careful, as they may break if you tug too hard. Draw up one side entirely, then draw up the adjacent side. Wriggle the gathers so they are evenly distributed (fig. 33). There is a choice of which side you now use. The top side will have threads showing more clearly than the underside; select which way up you prefer.

4. To prevent everything from unravelling, it is advisable to stitch the square on to a piece of backing fabric. Pin this indescribably scrumpled bit on a larger square of fabric, and firmly sew round the sides flattening the puckered edges as you go.

5. Cut strips of calico for the borders. By adding these to opposite sides first, then opening out and adding longer strips to the remaining sides, the bordering will be easy (fig. 34).

Now you can admire it, and I suspect that you will agree that until the borders are added, your sample did look a mess! A few seed pearls could be sewn on to the ruching, resembling glistening dew drops.

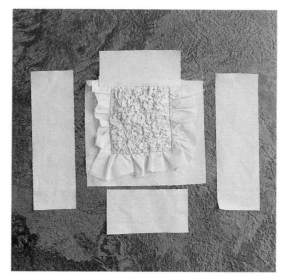

Fig 34

How about a ruched panel with bead work on an evening bag, placed on a box lid or made from silk forming the centre of a fabulous cushion as a wedding present ?

Ric-Rac Frill

Ric-rac is an undulating woven ribbon that can be used to decorate any edge, conceal seam joins, enhance plain areas; the Seminole Indians applied it to the bands in between their patchwork.

The same effect can be achieved with a folded strip (sides to middle) gathered in a diagonal manner before drawing up (fig. 35).

Gather by hand with a strong thread. With the machine, gather short lengths as the stress of ruching in a diagonal format will snap the thread.

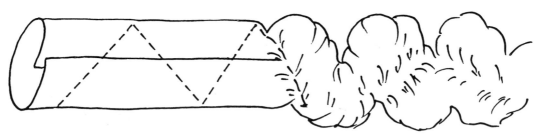

Fig 35

Tucked Circle Wall-hanging: (30″ diameter) edged in Prairie points with "Bow-Tie" appliqué centre (Jennie Rayment).

Trumpets or Cornets: in silk with ruched piping (Jennie Rayment).

Weaving with Fabric: Calico cushions with different stitching designs (Jennie Rayment).

Ruched Box: tucked sides and free machine quilting (Jennie Rayment).

Bias Tuck Calico Cushion: (Jennie Rayment).

Weaving with Fabric

The traditional craft of weaving is an ancient art form, and has been part of the fundamental structure of our daily lives for thousands of years. All manner of fibres have been and are used to create a cloth of some description. There has been a vogue in recent times to resurrect the ribbon weaving from the Victorian era.

During a flying visit to Los Angeles, I was ferreting round an interior design emporium and spotted a cushion that was made from woven and padded strips. It looked very similar to the method that I use for making bag handles. As a result, the aircraft could not fly back to England fast enough to let me get at the sewing machine and explore these ideas, and develop an easy way to incorporate "Weaving with Bag Handles" into my work.

****

Here is another textural creation that is really easy, and not only will you be able to weave with the strips, but the basic technique also makes exceedingly good handles!

Take the opportunity to introduce some colour. Experiment with space-dyed or contrasting threads when you stitch the woven bands, or change the backing material to a different shade. Vary the width and position of the strips and produce yet more exciting designs.

Remember that you can do anything you choose; it is not wrong, merely different! Once you understand the method, these ideas can be expanded in any way. There are many different weaving designs that may be translated in this fashion; look at books on ribbon weaving, study the structures of woven textiles and use the different rhythms and formation of the weaves to produce your own patterns using padded strips.

Measurements are suggested in the method which will construct a 8 - 9"
(20 - 23cm) panel. You may choose to alter the sizes.

Preparing the Woven Strips

You require ½ metre of fabric 45" (115cm) wide plus some small pieces
of 2oz. or 4oz. wadding/batting.

1. Cut 8 strips of 4 ½" (11cm) x 10"
(25cm). Do ensure that these are cut
across the calico (fig. 36).

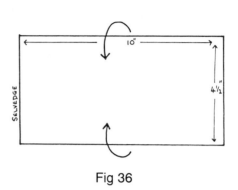

Fig 36

2. Press the long sides to the
centre, overlapping them by ¼" (.5cm)
(fig. 37).

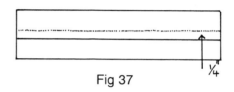

Fig 37

3. From the wadding, cut 8 strips
the length and width of the pressed
strip. Open the strip and lay the
wadding inside, as though you were
wrapping a present (fig. 38).

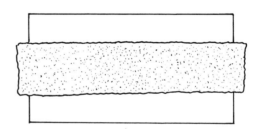

Fig 38

4. Pin all the layers together,
placing pins across the strip (tack first if
desired); then either by hand or
machine, stitch down the centre of the
strip (fig. 39); several rows of stitching
may be done to create a quilted effect
(see fig. 43). Repeat with all 8 strips.

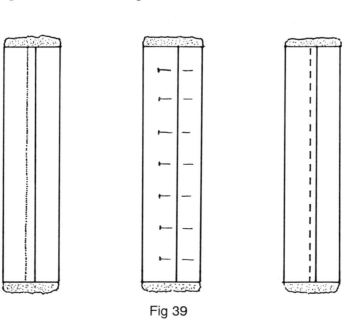

Fig 39

5. Trim any surplus wadding away and check that all 8 strips are the same length. Cut a 10" (25cm) square from the calico, place 4 strips along one edge of the square, setting in ½" (1cm) from each side and positioning them evenly; pin well. Machine or hand-stitch firmly along the edge using a ½" (1cm) seam allowance (fig. 40).

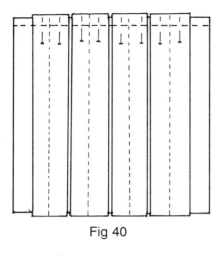

Fig 40

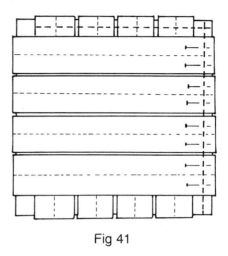

Fig 41

6. Repeat with the remaining 4 strips down the adjacent side, positioning equally as before, then sew firmly down the edge [½"(1cm) seam allowance] (fig. 41).

7. Weave together, under and over, as in basic weaving. Check the strips all lie parallel and are straight, before pinning firmly to the backing fabric, then sew down the remaining two sides, with the same seam allowance as before (fig. 42).

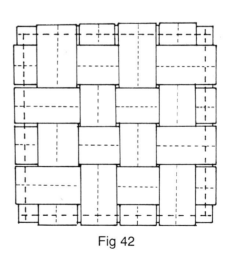

Fig 42

The panel is now ready to be framed with borders, and could be used for a cushion front, table mat, part of a textured wall-hanging, or set into another project.

Developing the Idea

Try experimenting with different widths of the padded strips, changing the colours, altering the weaving design, using a twin needle for a decorative stitch down the padded bands, or explore the range of fancy stitches on the machine. Embroideresses have such a wide variety of stitch techniques that each strip could be embellished in a different manner.

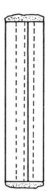 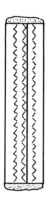   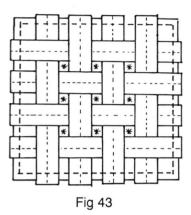

Fig 43

Change the backing square to a contrasting colour and space the strips further apart; this will be revealed through the gaps in the weave. Repeat this colour in thread on the woven bands (fig. 43).

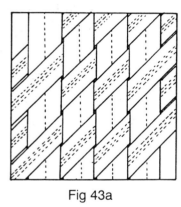

Fig 43a

Experiment with different weaving patterns, varying lengths for the diagonal, length or width of the backing material for the vertical weave (fig. 43a).

The method was originally called "Weaving with Bag Handles". I use these padded strips for handles, wrapping up wadding in the same fashion, but at the pressing stage, the raw edge is turned under by ¼" (.5cm), then ironed with the sides overlapping, as before (fig. 44). It makes very strong and robust handles that are easy to hold. [For making a quick bag - see the section on Finishing Techniques.]

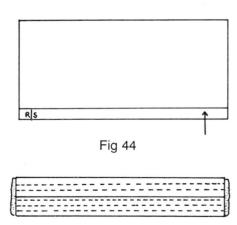

Fig 44

"Quilt-as-you-go"

This is a well known and useful technique, ideal for linking together sections of Texture work.

As the title indicates, the work can be quilted as it grows by placing the pieces on wadding. The quilting will not show as a surface decoration; it merely secures the fabric to the wadding.

I find that a layer of light-weight `sew-in' vilene underneath the fabric and above the wadding prevents the wadding from distorting and ensures greater accuracy in the piecing.

Using the "Quilt-as-you-Go" method, Prairie Points, Somerset Patchwork, piping, frayed layers, extra wadding and many other insertions may be included for an additional creative touch. The jacket and the landscape were both constructed in this manner.

Crazy Patchwork from random strips, Log Cabin and Pineapple Patchwork can also be worked with this method. The one drawback lies in the direction in which you can work. "Quilt-as-you-Go" only travels from the centre out or from the edge, either left to right, and vice versa, or from top to bottom of the worked piece. It is possible to catch oneself out and end up cheating, having to add a small amount of hand work or machine-applying one seam to correct the mistake. Although this can add a certain "je ne sais quoi" to the appearance, naturally - it was by design !

Seam allowances can be your own personal choice ¼" (.5cm) or a little more. Unless you are working to a given size, minor deviations in the seam allowance do not matter; nor does it really affect the ultimate result, if the seam lines are not very straight. After all this is your own creation!

Methods for "Quilt-as-you-Go"

Working from one Edge

    1. Cut wadding and light-weight 'sew-in' vilene, large enough for the completed creation (iron-on vilene is a total disaster as it can stick should you press the work!)

    2. Lay the first piece <u>right side up</u> along the top edge. Stitch within the seam allowance to prevent it from moving. Lay the next section <u>right side down/wrong side up</u>, pin if required and stitch through all the layers on the lower edge (fig. 45).

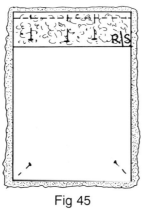

Fig 45

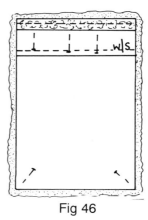

Fig 46

    3. Open out and finger-press flat; ironing can totally eradicate the wadding. Do check that the second section is smooth; the blunt end of your scissors or a ruler will help if there is not enough strength in your fingers (fig. 46).

    4. Add the next section, remembering to lay it <u>right side down</u> along the lower edge of the last piece. Pinning the layers as you go will help to keep the sections secure; now sew along the line through all the layers. Open out again and finger press flat (fig. 47).

    5. Continue in the same manner until the opposite side is reached; finally, stitch the outer edge of the last section (fig. 48).

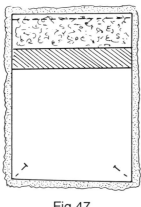

Fig 47

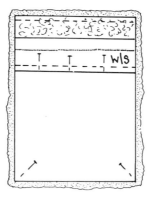
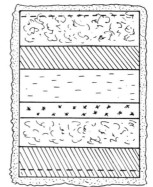

Fig 48

This quilted fabric can now be re-cut into any shape. Make it into a cushion, table-mat, hot water bottle cover or spectacle case. Lay a dressmaker's pattern on it and cut out clothing.

Adding Insertions to the Sample

Now you see how simple it is, try adding a few textural effects.

a. Once the first section has been laid down, before you add the next piece, fold up some Prairie Points,

Prairie Points are squares of fabric (size is irrelevant); fold once on the diagonal, fold again to form a triangle (fig. 49).

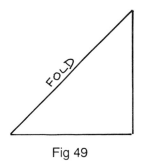

Fig 49

<u>OR</u> some Somerset Patches.

Somerset Patches are squares folded in half across the centre then the corners turned down forming a triangle. BUT the difference lies in the appearance: there is a line down the centre of the patch unlike Prairie Points where there is no centre line (fig. 50).

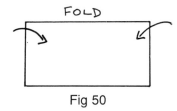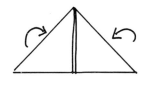

Fig 50

Overlap these patches ensuring the seam will pass through the junction (fig. 51).

b. Add some piping, see chapter on Finishing Techniques for the method.

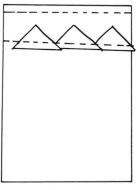

Fig 51

c.   Rip some fabric to make some frayed insertions. (Here it is allowed! See page 13.) Tear thin strips, insert them, then fray to the desired length. Trim back, if necessary. Several torn strips can be added to produce a thick fringe.

d.   Ruche some fabric by gathering opposite sides, possibly fold in half and stitch together. See chapter on Ruching for further ideas.

e.   Set a large satin stitch on the machine, then meander at random over the fabric, altering the density of stitch. This creates a "thread" textured material, which can be cut up and inserted into the work. Some of the space-dyed machine threads look most attractive.

f.   Why not include pieces of hand embroideries, odd remnants of textured sections, other types of fabric in the same colour tone, lace, ribbons and decorative braids? Nearly any scrap can be inserted into the work. You could even have a tassel!

It is preferable to stitch any textural supplement before the next layer is added. Sew within the seam allowance then when the next section is attached, the stitching will not show (fig. 52).

It seems a waste of valuable time to do this anchoring, but the bits seem to have a life of their own and a little demon shifts them while you are not looking.

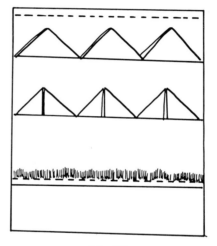

Fig 52

g.   Include extra padding before attaching the next section. Lift up the last piece, lay the padding under, pin down to prevent it shifting, stitch down before adding the next layer.

Keep going; you can add whatever relevant creations you desire. Coloured fringeing could be grass and a ruched section may be a rocky cluster. Adding piping or folded squares gives more textural dimensions to the calico sample.

Working from the Centre

"Quilt-as-you-Go" may be worked from the centre, from either a vertical, horizontal or diagonal strip or from a central shape.

With a strip it is easiest to position the central section first, then work out towards each side. Remember to pin and keep the pieces flat. Stitch the outer edges of any diagonal samples to prevent the cloth stretching (fig. 53).

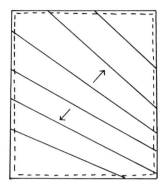

Fig 53

A central shape can lead to a few difficulties, although it depends on the structure.

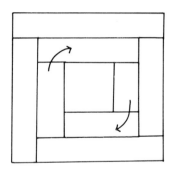

Fig 54

With a standard geometric form such as a square, sew in a clockwise or anti-clockwise pattern, remembering to open and flatten the layers as you go (fig. 54). Be systematic!

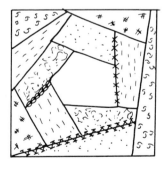

Fig 55

Using an abstract shape, take care to check that you cover all the raw edges when adding the next layer. Any small holes can be concealed with a little embroidery or a sneaky bit of hand stitching, (fig 55). This may even improve the whole appearance!

To sum up, this technique is both simple and effective; it is quick to produce and so useful to have at your fingertips! I could wax lyrical on the subject, so perhaps the next book will develop the theme!

Delving
into the
Bias

When I first started investigating the potential of texturing surfaces, I played only with the straight grain of the material. But when I tried the bias grain, new horizons were opened.

Initially, I tried tucking down the bias without really thinking what would happen. Then, when I flexed the tucks, they did not twist as before; they rolled flat, just like the centres of Cathedral Window patchwork. It is amazing how blinkered one can be! If I had thought at all, the edges of Cathedral Windows only roll because they are on the bias grain.

From this beginning, a whole range of textural ideas has sprung. One of the cushions that is always popular features this effect; for some reason it appeals to everyone - particularly gentlemen. They appear to appreciate this textured design especially in the calico.

Having said that, the entire male population will now get bombarded with Bias Tuck cushions in various ways!

The potential of this technique is discussed at the end of the method - there are many possibilities for extending and interpreting the design.

There is only one rule to be followed:

Strips for Bias Tucks have to be cut on the bias.

Preparing the Bias Strips

To make a cushion front approximately 1 metre of calico is required 40 - 45" (115cm) wide, plus ½ metre of 4oz. wadding/batting.

Cut off 15 - 16" (38 - 40cm) from the metre (it is much easier to cut the bias strips from a smaller section).

1. Use the rotary cutter and ruler to cut the strips. Position the ruler so the 45° line is on the selvedge; if your ruler lacks this line, try using the lines on the cutting mat, and lining up the 45° line imprinted on the board with the selvedge (fig. 56).

2. Make the first cut diagonally across the calico. From this bias edge measure 5" (12cm), and cut a strip; keep cutting until you have 5 - 6 pieces. Sufficient strips have to be cut to cover the backing square.

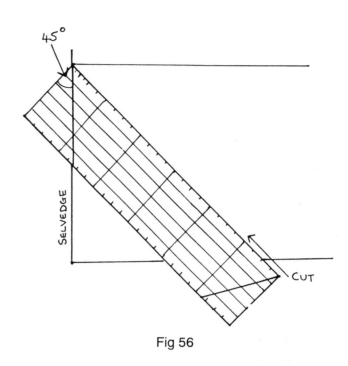

Fig 56

3. Cut a 15" (38cm) square for backing the design from the remaining fabric. Also cut a square of 4oz. wadding/batting slightly larger than this. Pin the four corners of the backing square to the wadding, pins positioned diagonally, pointing outwards.

4. Press the bias strips - sides to middle (just touching not over-lapping), and starting from the central strip cover the backing square with these pressed bands with the raw edges on the underside. Pin well through all the layers and trim strips level with the backing square (fig. 57).

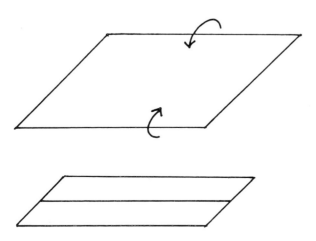
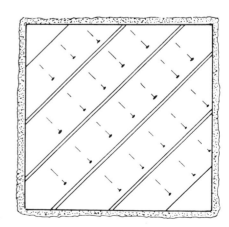

Fig 57

5. Using ½" (1cm) seam allowance, sew up and down all the edges of the bias panels. If using a machine, lengthen the stitch to 3 or slightly longer than usual, as the wadding and layers of material will contract the stitch length. By hand, use a small firm back stitch (fig. 58).

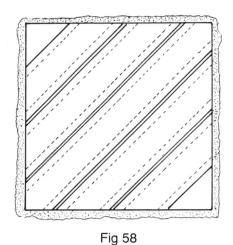

Fig 58

6. Open the tucks, and in the channels add a fancy machine stitch, hand embroidery, ribbon or lace. This will be revealed when the pleats are rolled back (fig. 59).

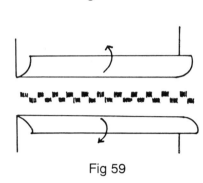

Fig 59

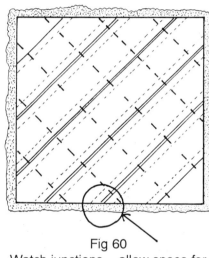

Fig 60
Watch junctions – allow space for seam allowance.

7. Close the tucks again; carefully mark equal divisions, approximately 2 ½" (6.5cm) across the square on the opposing diagonal; use a hard (H) pencil, or a vanishing pen (fig. 60).

Check that the pen will vanish. Some products return, especially if you have pre-washed the fabric, as the residue of the detergent can chemically affect the ink.

Ensure that these lines cross the sewn ones, allowing for a seam allowance round the outside of the panel.

8. Sew along these lines, either by hand or machine; a grid of squares will be formed.

9. Roll back the edges of the stitched squares - these tucks will curve back as in Cathedral Window patchwork; pin if desired to hold flat before you stitch them down (fig. 61).

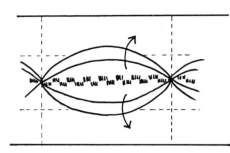
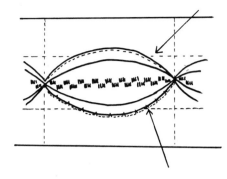

Fig 61

10. Sew on the outer edge of rolled tuck; use a running, blind hem, fine satin stitch, or any hand stitch. Use a matching or contrasting coloured thread.

Invisible thread will conceal a multitude of mistakes. Remember to have cotton thread on the bottom bobbin.

The settings for a very fine blind hem stitch are :
1 - stitch length, 1 - stitch width.
Use the normal straight stitch presser foot

Bernina users - re-align the needle position to the centre.

Open the tucks in the whole squares only, and leave the tucks in the part-formed squares closed. A series of "bobbles" or ovals will now appear and the original embroidery will show through the spaces. Where there are no "bobbles", the tucked edge can be secured with a straight stitch (fig. 62).

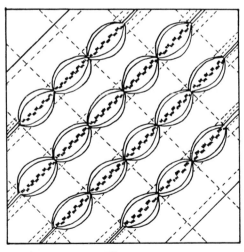

Fig 62

11. Trim off any uneven edges and square up the design.

This is now ready to be completed in your chosen manner.
[See Finishing Section for further information.]

Further Experiments with the Bias

Change the size of the "bobbles" by altering the width of the lines running on the opposing diagonal; you could have large and/or small ones. (Less than 1 ½" (4cm) in length is difficult to roll back.)

By anchoring the tucks down in an uneven format, you can mix the sizes of the ovals (fig. 63).

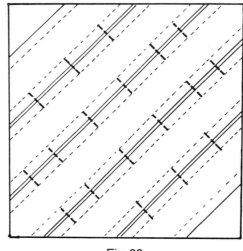

Fig 63

Try catching the rolled edges down in only one or two places and not all the way, or catch at the mid-point with a French knot.

Roll open only one side of the tuck, or twist as it rolls back.

The bias strips can be laid on the vertical or horizontal on the backing fabric.

The backing material could be a patterned cloth, arranging the "bobbles" to roll back and reveal parts of the print. Striped designs may be used. Some fabrics have a colour wash in graduated tones and different shades will be revealed through the windows. Strips of material can be laid in the channels, which will have a similar effect.

Construct the bias sections in chintz, lay them on to silk. Experiment with different types of materials.

Imagine all the possibilities!

Play on!!

Bias Tuck in a Square

1. Cut three squares the same size. Fold two in half diagonally; lay on to the third square and pin well (fig 64).

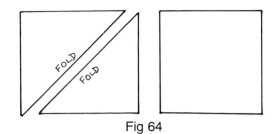

Fig 64

2. Stitch ½″ (1cm) seam down either side of the centre folds. Open channel for embroidery etc. Anchor the folds at some point - see previous method (fig. 65).

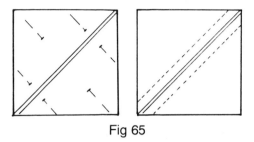

Fig 65

3. Roll back the fold and stitch (fig. 66).

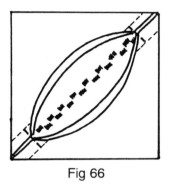

Fig 66

This could be inserted into a corner on a quilt, used in a pelmet or any border design. Four panels would make a cushion cover.

Inserting a Single Bias Tuck Band

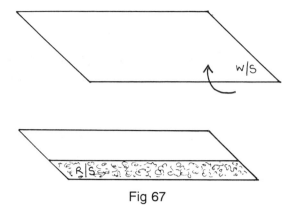

1. Cut 2 strips of bias as before. Press 1" (2.5cm) seam over. Position both strips on an additional straight cut strip, butting the folds (fig. 67), pin well.

Fig 67

Fig 67

2. Stitch ½" (1cm) from the folds through all the layers. Embroidery may be included in the channel. Secure the folds. Roll back and catch down (fig. 68).

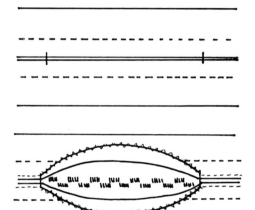

Fig 68

Try this on a tie-back, a waistcoat, a belt or a jacket sleeve - it is not dissimilar to the Elizabethan slashed sleeves. [Refer to the Jacket section.]

It looks good, it's easy
and it's different !!

46

"Trumpets and Cornets"

Originally this technique had no name but has collected its title along the way. "Trumpets" or "Cornets" is infinitely preferable to "Squashed Prairie Points" although this is what they are!

Continuing with the explorations into the effects of a bias roll, this idea grew from a folded strip. It had occurred to me that it could be useful if the Bias Tuck design turned a corner. I tried and it didn't! Unfortunately, a triangle of excess material remained, so in desperation I flattened it. To my amazement the sides of this shape rolled and it had an intriguing textural form. Would it be possible to condense this initial strip so these triangles met at the centre? The possibilities seemed endless.

Like all things, another day when the house went to pot; we had to play! Since teaching Patchwork, I have discovered all kinds of sneaky tricks to convince the nearest and dearest that I have been hard at work `doing' the housework. There is nothing like a few track lines from the Hoover on the carpet; pictures knocked slightly askew and merrily boiling saucepans containing only water and a stock cube to preserve the illusion that one has been frantically busy all day. The Microwave rules OK !

Finally, after many devious and complex experiments, a wastepaper bin full of scraps, I cracked the technique. Eureka! Instead of a highly complex piece of fabric manipulation, this magic method is a piece of cake.

Composing the Cornet

    1. Cut 8 equal squares from the calico; these can be of any size, but 6" (15cm) is a good starting point.

Use the rotary cutter and ruler to cut a 6" (15cm) strip from the material; subdivide into the squares by turning the ruler and cutting vertically instead of horizontally.

    2. Fold 4 of the squares into triangles, press gently; using a long stitch length or small tacking stitch, baste the edges together. Sew within the ¼" (.5cm) seam allowance (fig. 69).

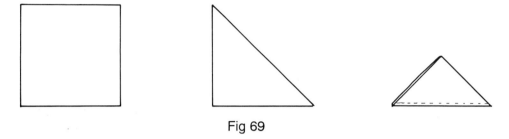

Fig 69

    3. Lay one of the squares on the side of an unfolded square, stitch on the same line as before to hold it, then lay another square on top (forming a sandwich); stitch the layers together with ¼" (.5cm) seam (fig. 70).

 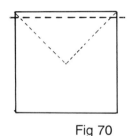 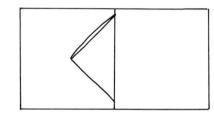

Fig 70

    4. Repeat this operation; you will now have two sets of triangles trapped in four squares.

    5. Open one set of squares and place the remaining two triangles at right-angles to the central section, overlapping at the mid-point by the seam allowance. Baste as before to stabilise all the triangles (fig. 71).

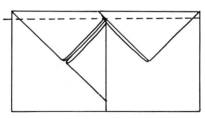

Fig 71

Watch that all the openings are towards the centre - it is easy to make a mistake!

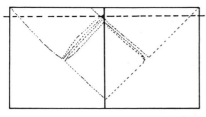

Fig 72

6. Open the remaining piece (with the triangle insertion) and lay on top. Reverse this triangle so it lies in the opposite direction to the other central one. They will slot together (fig. 72).

Check that you have all the openings in the same place i.e. towards the middle.

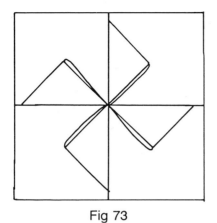

Fig 73

7. Pin the layers together and sew all along the edge. Change the machine needle to 90/100 as there are so many layers. Open out and lay flat; the triangles are all inserted between the squares (fig. 73).

Due to the thickness of the fabrics, the centre point may not be quite accurate. A covered button or attractive bead conceals any misdemeanour!

8. Lift the triangles and flatten (fig. 74) and there it is: "Cornets or Trumpets". With a small stitch catch the corners to hold the shape flat (fig. 74a).

The edges will all roll back à la Cathedral Windows/Bias Tuck.

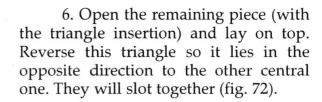

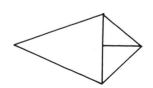

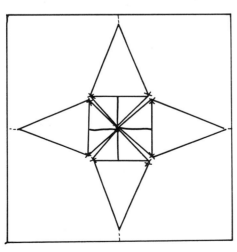

Fig 74a

Fig 74

You may wish to quilt the sample to add additional texture. Either quilt before stitching the corners of the triangles or after all the edges have been rolled. [For quilting hints - see Finishing Techniques.]

9. Roll back the edges and stitch down through all the layers; refer to the Bias Tuck for stitching techniques (fig. 75).

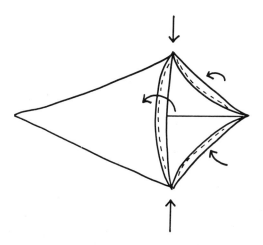 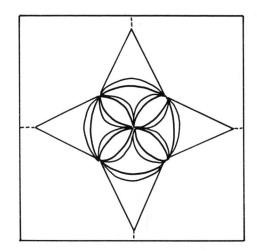

Fig 75

There are many different ideas you can now explore:-

a. Cover the central seam line with a triangular scrap of fabric. All the edges at the top of the "Cornet" will roll to cover the raw edges of the inserted scrap (fig. 76).

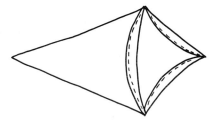

Fig 76

b. Insert a Prairie Point - see "Quilt -as-you-Go" chapter (fig. 77).

c. Stuff the triangles with a small quantity of wadding, or even some pot pourri; then sew the edge down to hold the filling in place.

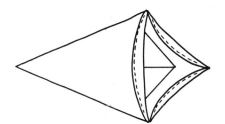

Fig 77

d. Do all three ideas for a really effective piece of textural work.

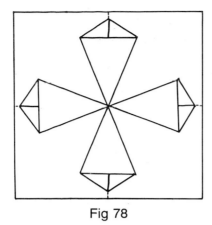

Fig 78

Arrange the entire concept in a different manner, with all the openings away from the centre; This makes a cross not dissimilar to the Viking sign of blessing on rune stones (fig. 78).

Yet again, the "Cornets" can be padded, rolled and have various insertions.

Additional Ideas with the "Cornet"

There is no reason why these triangular sections cannot be inserted into any seam. Try sandwiching them between two triangles, then the "Cornet" will be on the diagonal (fig. 79). You could have eight, radiating out from the centre.

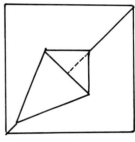

Fig 79

These folded triangles can be any size; there is no reason why they have to be the same as the squares. Try small "Cornets" inserted in large squares; they can be positioned at any distance (fig. 80).

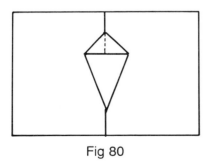

Fig 80

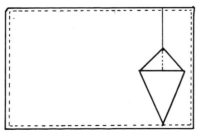

Fig 81

Introduce into a tablemat for holding the napkin (fig. 81). Use as pockets for an Advent Calendar. Large "Cornets" could be part of a shoe tidy, or a child's wall-hanging to hold little toys. Small "Trumpets" could be a decorative feature on the shoulders of fashion garments. Explore the effectiveness of this shape as florets, similar to Bluebells or Delphiniums. (Stretching a point I know, but why not ?)

Once again, the choice is yours: just remember that you selected to have a covered button in the centre, or decided to have the "Trumpets" at odd angles; this was your personal design decision and not a mistake.

****

<u>The Triangle Cornet</u>

A rare musical instrument !!

This is technically half of a "Cornet" and has equally as many variations on the theme.

1. Cut a 6" (15cm) square in half on the diagonal forming two triangles to make two Triangle Cornets (fig. 82).

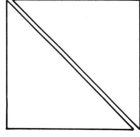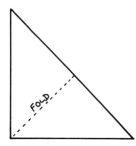

Fig 82

2. Fold right sides together, stitch the diagonal, turn inside out (fig. 83).

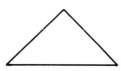

Fig 83

3. Lay this shape between two squares, basting on to the first square before adding the other square, as in Trumpet method (fig. 84).

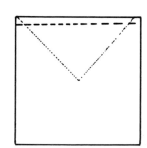

Fig 84

4. Open out, squash the shape (fig. 85).

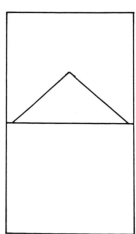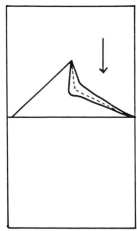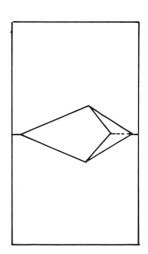

Fig 85

Developing the Design

Secure the corners of the shape to the base material - roll the edges.

The flap can be turned in either direction, anchored with a bead; stitched underneath to retain the shape and emphasise the texture; stitched on top to isolate the point (fig. 86).

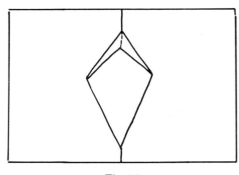

Fig 86

Insert the Triangle Cornet between triangles (fig. 87) - eight T/Cs make a Star Design.

Explore the effect, sandwiched within different geometric forms.

Alternate the Triangle Cornets reversing every other one. Alternate with Trumpets, one up - one down!

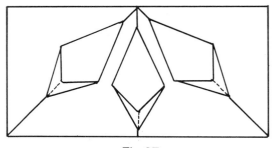

Fig 87

'In creating, the only hard thing's to begin; A grass blade's no easier to make than an oak'.
James Russell Lowell 1848

And you are only making a Triangle Cornet!

For the finale - it has to be

The Trumpet Voluntary!

As you will discover when you start to play with folded shapes, there are many other variations on a theme. This one is formed by re-folding the original "Prairie Point" in half to create a further textural insert.

   1. Construct a "Prairie Point" (see "Quilt-as-you-go"). Re-fold the shape down the centre, folding A to C and B to C. Baste or tack the layers together to prevent any movement of the folds (fig. 88).

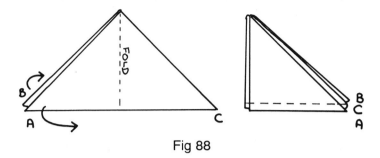

Fig 88

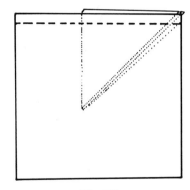

   2. Sandwich between any two equal squares or triangles. Pin the layers together and stitch with the usual ¼" (.5cm) seam allowance (fig. 89).

Fig 89

   3. Open out and pull shape down from the top then flatten (fig. 90).

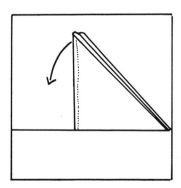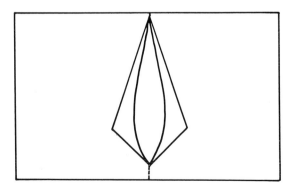

Fig 90

Catch the corners on to the base material either by a stitch or small bead. Experiment with rolling the edges. Place some padding underneath the shape before stitching in place. (See colour photographs.)

Lifted Star

The Lifted Star Patchwork (sometimes called the Raised Star) has been included in this book as it looks very ornamental in one colour, most attractive in several colours, and is easy to make; the only drawback lies in the fact that it uses a vast amount of fabric.

Although actual design of this patchwork greatly resembles Somerset or Folded Patchwork, the construction is completely different. It is preferable to use the sewing machine because there are many layers which make the design difficult to hand sew. (Somerset can be done more easily by hand.)

As the Star is composed on eight lines, the final structure is octagonal, as opposed to Somerset which can be circular. Also this Patchwork has the same number of patches on each line, unlike the former; this increases in quantity of pieces as it radiates out.

Both patchworks require a large amount of squares to be pre-cut; it is advantageous to use the rotary cutter, mat and ruler. All the squares for the Lifted Star have to be pressed beforehand so the preparation work can be time-consuming, but after this the design will grow quickly.

For a rapid textural effect that appears highly impressive, this design is hard to beat. It is ideal as a gift and will delight the recipient, who will be amazed at your professional skill. Also you may wish to suggest that dry cleaning the Star would be preferable, as it is constructed from so many layers of fabric that it will take a long time to dry.

As before the measurements are given; further ideas for selecting colours and design development are included at the end of the method.

Preparing the Pieces

11" (28cm) - 12" (30cm) Star

Remember to iron the fabric beforehand, then fold into four, lining up the selvedges with the central fold before you make the first cut.

1. Cut 48 x 6" (15cm) squares in the calico, using the rotary cutter to cut a 6" (15cm) strip from the material, re-cut the strip vertically into the 6" squares.

Press all the pieces into 3" (7.5cm) squares. Fold in half along the straight grain of the fabric (into a rectangle), fold again to form a smaller square (fig. 91).

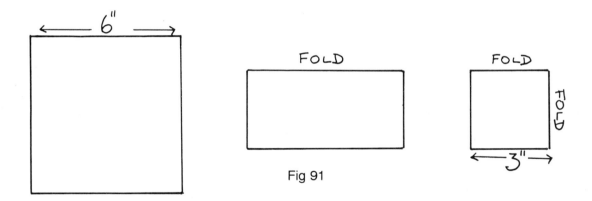

Fig 91

Alternative method - saves some material!

As you will discover, this Patchwork eats calico; there is an alternative method of cutting out the squares. Cut the 6" (15cm) strip; cut off as many 6" (15cm) squares as possible; stop when the remainder of the strip measures less than 12" (30cm); divide this in half. The pieces must measure 6" (15cm) in one direction. These odd-sized scraps are folded with the shorter edge on the right-side, then pressed so they measure 3" (7.5cm) square, with the shorter length on the outside (fig. 92).

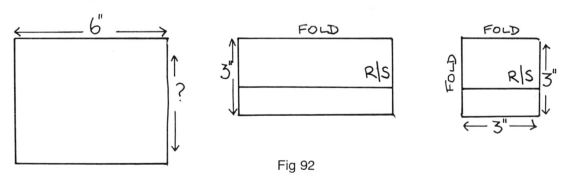

Fig 92

2. Cut a 14" (35cm) - 15" (38cm) square from the calico to back the design. Other material can be used but do ensure that it has a firm weave as a fine fabric does not support the weight of the Star and will distort.

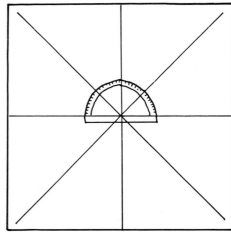

Fig 93

3. Draw the eight major lines of the compass, extending the lines across the whole of the backing piece. This can be done by folding the material and pressing the creases, but it is more accurate to use a protractor and mark equal divisions of 45° (fig. 93).

Find the centre of the square (fold into four, forming a smaller square and finger press the midpoint), place the protractor on this mark, lining the little cross on the middle of the protractor with the centre mark. Now mark off the 0°, 45°, 90°, 135°, 180° degree points, turn the protractor round and mark the 45°, 90°, 135° points. Join all the lines through the centre mark, extending across the entire fabric. The lines need to be long.

4. Complete the preparations by cutting a 1" (2.5cm) square from either the corner of one of the pre-cut squares or from a scrap of calico.

Method for Sewing the Star.

1. Place the 1" square in the centre of the drawn lines; this prevents the lines showing through any gap in the pieces (fig. 94). Divide the 48 squares into 8 sets of six squares, one set for every line.

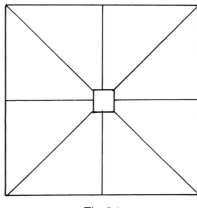

Fig 94

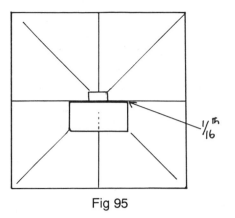

Fig 95

2. Select one of the lines, open out one of the squares, and line up the pressed crease with the drawn line, positioning the fold of the rectangle ⅟₁₆" (.1cm) - a fraction away from the centre (fig. 95).

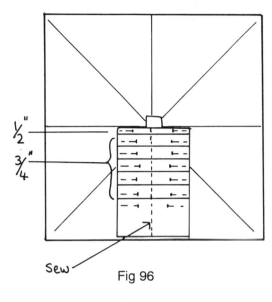

Sew

Fig 96

3. Place the remaining five squares down the same line, space apart using the measurements shown in the diagram. Pin all the sections firmly through to the backing fabric (fig. 96).

By replacing the pins with Sellotape, or similar, the sections can be secured to the backing material; this saves time and is just as accurate.

4. Stitch out from the centre, following the creased line; sew to the end of the sections (fig. 97).

5. Repeat on all the remaining lines, using the same accurate spacing of each piece.

Watch carefully that the sections are not caught up in the sewing; push the previous sets firmly to one side before positioning the next one.

6. Begin to fold. These squares are accurately folded to the back on the diagonal (fig. 97). Take care to fold correctly.

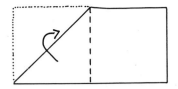

Fig 97

Start at any section. Fold the right side over the left side. Continue folding and interlacing the folded squares (fig. 98) until the last set is reached.

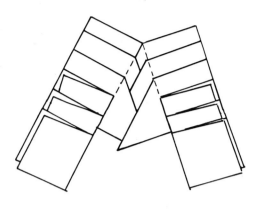

Fold the final set obliquely - not on the true diagonal. Ensure that they overlap.

If this last set is not "mis-folded", the Star will not lie flat.

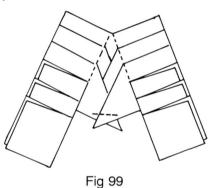

Fig 99

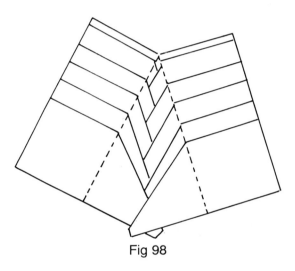

Fig 98

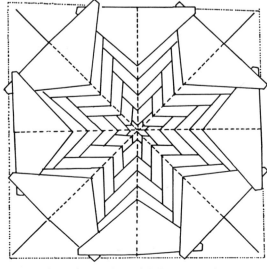

Lifted Star when folding complete

7. After folding the design, systematically undo each section; secure each folded set of squares through to the backing material with a few stitches on the lower edge (fig. 99). (Little inquisitive fingers may destroy your creation!)

Check the points of the Star sections; they should all be equal measurements from the centre, or the octagonal effect will be lost.

8. Now the folding is complete, machine round the outer edge of the octagon to hold the folded design in place.

If you place the rotary rule so the ¼" (.5cm) line passes through the tips of the Star, then draw a line from tip to tip, this will give you a sewing line and a positioning line for adding the triangles to convert the octagon into a square.

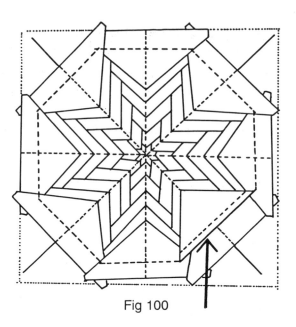

Fig 100

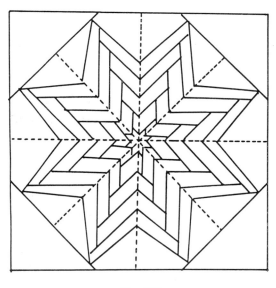

Fig 101

9. Cut 2 extra 6"(15cms) squares, divide on the diagonal forming 4 triangles. Place these so the side of the triangle is aligned with the drawn line, pin and stitch along the edge, using a ¼"(.5cm) seam allowance (fig. 100).

(These triangles are technically too large, sometimes the added extra aids the "squaring up"!!)

Stitch all 4 triangles in place, placing one on every other section (fig 101).

When the triangles are laid flat to make the final square, the seam should run through the tip of the folded section.

10. Trim off any excess fabric and "square up" the design. Press gently, then complete as preferred. See Chapter on Finishing Techniques.

Any small gaps in the centre of the Star can be covered with an attractive button, bead or some embroidery, or even a small tassel if the Lifted Star is to be used as a lid.

Extensions to Design

1. Explore the use of colour in the Star:-

a. Try cutting 8 squares of 6 colours, or 16 x 3 colours, or 24 x 2 colours; these can be arranged in a sequence on each line.

b. Fascinating spiral patterns could be constructed with colour. (See colour photographs.)

c. Change the colour sequence in alternate rows, then change the folding pattern. Instead of folding right over left consistently, change to alternating the folding (i.e. right over left then left over right etc.); this will have the effect of making some colours seem more dominant than others.

2. How about changing the size of the basic squares:-

a. Try cutting 3" (7.5cm) squares and halving all the spacing measurements. Leave the ¹⁄₁₆" (.1cm) intact, but divide all the others in half; ¼", ⅜", ⅜" etc. (.5cm, 1cm, 1cm).

b. Cut 4" (10cm) basic squares, then divide all the measurements pro rata (⅔rds of the set spacings).

c. The Star can be increased by adding larger squares to the same lines, but this becomes very heavy. This would need a larger piece of backing fabric to begin with.

d. Change the folding design by folding forwards. When the last set is mis-folded, a gap will appear forming a further textural effect (fig. 101a). This could be enhanced by constructing the final squares from different coloured oblongs. (See colour photographs.)

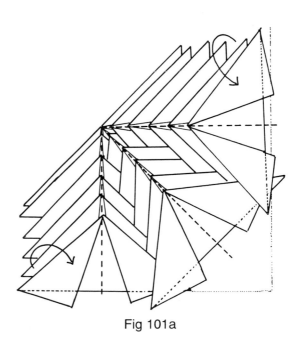

Fig 101a

Experiment with different angles at the centre by dividing the centre into equal divisions of 30° and having twelve lines (fig. 102). This will require 4 x 6" (15cm) squares for each line; the folding and the spacing has to be adjusted.

Change the spacings to ⅟₁₆"; 1½"; 1¼"; 1¼" (1cm, 4cm, 3cm, 3cm).

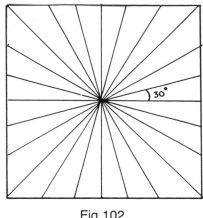

Fig 102

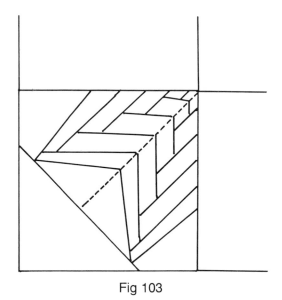

Fig 103

Insert a quarter of the Star on a corner, creating a texture in the border (fig. 103).

This design makes wonderful cushions. In the smaller size it is very good for the lid of a hat box, needlework box or basket. Made up in Christmas fabrics, it will be a stunning wall-hanging.

Hatbox, Lifted Star and Napkins: box displays the "Trumpet Voluntary" and "Bow-Tie" with pin tucked inserts. Napkin with frayed edges and padded napkin rings (Jennie Rayment).

Landscape: (24" x 18") in microwave dyed fabric, "Quilt-as-you-go" technique with a variety of textured surfaces (Jennie Rayment).

Knotted Strips and Tucks Bag: Plaited handles created with padded strips (Jennie Rayment).

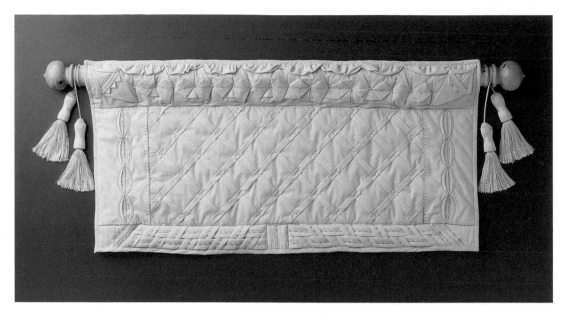

Calico Headboard: (20" x 36") with Crossing Tucks central panel, Origami Twist and Triangle Cornets are among the techniques used (Shelagh Jarvis).

Quilt: (84" x 60") textured and embroidered calico panels (Shelagh Jarvis).

From Knits to Knots

Did you think that this book was about sewing?
It is but there are times when knitting and knotting will give just that little added extra!

Knitted material has a splendid texture, and can be used in the centre of Cathedral Window patchwork, Origami Twist or the "Bow-Tie". It can be inserted into cushions, as panels in clothing or even used to make rugs and table-mats.

No one thought you were eccentric until now. But when your husband arrives home and discovers you solemnly cutting a square of fabric into a long strip, then winding it into a ball and knitting with it, he will think that you have reached the point of no return. It may possibly cross his mind that you have squandered the housekeeping and cannot afford any wool, so had to resort to an alternative.

Just accept the fact that you are , like all of us, charmingly potty; but here is a way to use up all the old scraps that have been hoarded for years. 1960's crimplenes, lengths of furnishing fabrics, chintzes, those vibrantly coloured pieces that were "a good idea at the time" - in fact any fabric will knit. You could convert all those polythene carrier bags into a knitted section for a fully washable, wipe-able and hard-wearing mat!

Knitting Technique

Cut large rectangles or squares from the material, round off the corners, then starting at one edge, cut a ½" (1cm) strip, round and round the shape. Keep going until the centre is reached, wind into a ball and begin to knit (fig. 104).

Beware: the fabric will reduce to approximately ⅛th of its area when knitted up.

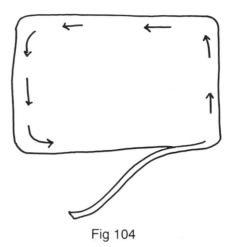

Fig 104

Thick steel, alloy, well polished wood or plastic needles can be used; these are preferable to fine ones as the thickness of the strips forms a firm and dense weave.

Cast on loose stitches, and keep the tension/gauge fairly slack; fabric lacks the same elasticity as wool with the exception of the stretch materials, e.g. crimplene. If the strip breaks, either weave in the next length or tie a knot in it.

Basic garter stitch (plain knitting) works well producing a knobbly texture, although you could experiment with other knitting designs.

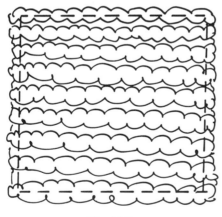

Fig 105

When you have knitted sufficient for the desired space, straighten the section and reinforce the outer edge by stitching round on the sewing machine (fig. 105). This prevents it all from unravelling should any trimming be required.

One of the advantages of this technique is to break up large colour masses and diffuse into a pleasing haze. It also will condense the colour, yet the areas of light and shadow within the weave reflect the texture. Using glazed cotton (chintz) creates an interesting weave as the sheen glistens when twisted in the knitting.

As suggested at the beginning, there are many places where knitted fabrics can be used.

Gather up all those ancient materials, cut into the strips and start knitting.

Create a textural and tactile panel for a cushion. This could even be the new carpet for the living room! Achieve a rapid result by employing the children, as it is ideal for small fingers, even if they only wind the ball.

Cathedral window with knitted calico insertions

****

Plaiting and Knotting

Add other textures by plaiting strips together or by tying a few knots in a band. Tie-backs for curtains can be made from plaited fabric, using the curtain material or complimentary colours. Create comfortable and strong handles for all kinds of bags from either twists or plaits - maybe even a knotted band for that unusual finishing touch.

Constructing a Plait

The width of the finished plait will depend on the intended use. Tie-backs need fairly thick, well- padded bands, and it would be preferable to turn the raw edge under as the strip will twist in the construction; the width of plaits for handles and straps will relate to the size of the bag to which they are attached.

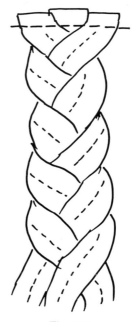

1. Make 3 long padded strips [use the technique described in "Weaving with Fabric" section].

Plaiting contracts the length by approximately ⅔rds

2. Lay the strips together, the outer two set fractionally over the centre one; stitch to secure.

3. Plait the strips - right over centre, left over centre etc (fig. 106).

Fig 106

Place the presser foot on the start to anchor the bands while you plait

4. Stitch the ends together before inserting.

There is no reason why ribbons or threads cannot be incorporated into the piece, or why the strips have to be the same size, thickness and colour.

Investigate other types of plait - try different plaiting weaves with more strips.

Plaits could be used as a decorative edge for a cushion. Attach plaited piping cords and braids to pelmets echoing the textured tie-backs. How about a central panel for a cushion? Create a matching hair band or belt to complete your fashion accessories!

Knotting

Knotted strips could be employed in a similar vein. Short lengths with either one or two knots could be inserted into some textured work; the knots could be arranged in a sequence or an abstract pattern. Experiment with different types of knots, or possibly tie several knots together.

A panel of knotted strips could be embellished with bead work, or embroidered as further ornamentation.

****

Frayed Fabrics

Rip the cloth for an interesting frayed textural insert (see "Quilt-as-you-Go section) or fringe the fibres for a decorative finishing touch.

Create some attractive table linen by fringeing the edges of tablecloths and napkins then secure the threads with machine stitching.

Tear the material to the desired size. Position the presser foot approximately ½" (1cm) from the ripped edge; select a decorative stitch, possibly one of the stretch stitches like the honeycomb (if your machine does not have any fancy stitches, use two narrow rows of fine straight stitches instead). Then sew round the article keeping the presser foot at the correct measurement from the edge of the fabric. Fray the threads by pulling the long fibres out. Stop the fraying two or three fibres from the stitching line (fig. 106a).

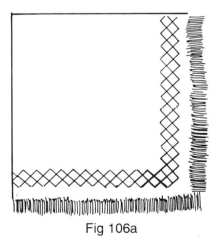

Fig 106a

If you choose to use one of the heavier embroidery stitches, placing paper underneath the material will prevent any buckling of the cloth. The paper will tear away easily afterwards, leaving a residue under the threads which will soften with wear and washing.

Slashed Fabric

There are several quilters and embroiderers who specialise in this technique and produce some amazing textural effects. It can look stunning when colour is introduced.

One method to create a slashed section is to stitch a pad of different coloured fabrics together, or use several layers of one fabric. Sew through the layers on the straight grain in a square grid format (fig. 107).

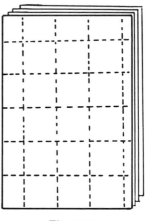

Use a fairly firm material as a base with lighter weight fabrics on top. You may choose to have the darkest colour on the top with the brighter hues underneath. These will be revealed when the material is slashed.

Fig 107

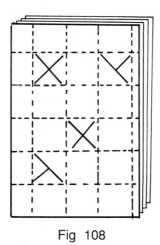

Fig 108

Once the pad has been stitched, the layers of fabric should be cut on the bias/diagonal (this is necessary or the material will fray away completely). Snip through some or all of the layers, cutting on the diagonal. It is unnecessary to slash all the diagonals, try different effects. You may choose to leave some parts of the grid intact (fig. 108).

The pad is then washed, and placed in the tumble dryer. This causes the cut sections to roll outwards for maximum textural effect (fig. 109).

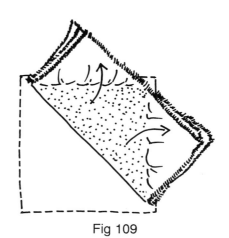

For that little additional extra touch - you could knit, plait, slash or even fray it!!

Fig 109

Why Knot!

68

Origami Twist

Origami is the art of folding paper and it is uncertain whether it originated from the Japanese, Koreans or the Chinese. The name derives from Japanese *ori* meaning fold, *kami* meaning paper. (*Kami* becomes *gami* when linked).

Technically speaking, no cutting, gluing or decoration of the paper is allowed. Although rules can be broken, I try not to cut the fabric; glue is cheating and any decoration is optional.

Many of the folding techniques originating in this ancient art of Origami can be translated into fabric. Naturally, material is not as stiff as paper; there is an added advantage - any fold that is on the diagonal or bias will roll back; therefore a simple origami design can be extended by using this effect.

One of my students, Margot Abrahams, takes great delight in sending me small samples of new ideas. She always omits the instructions, leaving me to fathom them out for myself. This usually results in extra levels of dust in the house and ironing piling up by the foot, as I have to work out the method and then discover a way to teach the concept.

This particular design can be made from one piece of material, or it can be made from four squares stitched together. In the further developments at the end of the chapter, you will see many exciting possibilities for extending the idea.

Technique for Origami Twist

You will require four equal squares of calico, any size, but for this example try 8" (20cm). Stitch the pieces together, forming a larger square; the seam allowance is irrelevant - for argument's sake use ¼" (.5cm). Press the seams open to reduce bulk.

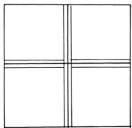

1. Fold the square in half on the diagonal, right sides together; press the edge. Open out, fold gently on the crease so the wrong sides are together, forming a triangle (fig. 110a).

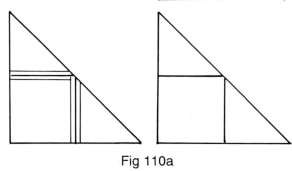

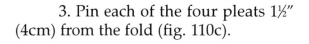

Fig 110a

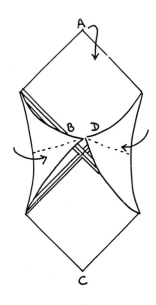

2. Lift A, hold B and tuck in; as there is a crease it will tuck in easily. Repeat with D; finger press the seams. All the points are gathered together (fig. 110b).

3. Pin each of the four pleats 1½" (4cm) from the fold (fig. 110c).

Only pin half way along the pleat.

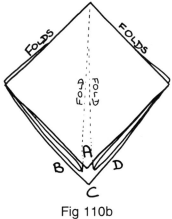

Fig 110b

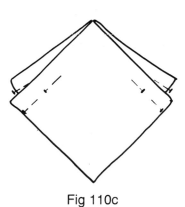

Fig 110c

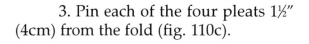

Fig 111

4. Gently open out and push all the pleats in <u>one</u> direction. The centre will begin to twist; it will need some persuasion to lie flat.

Manoeuvre the centre, ensuring it lies on the diagonal; the pins may have to be removed to permit this (fig. 111).

The centre can be secured on all four corners with a small stitch (fig. 112).

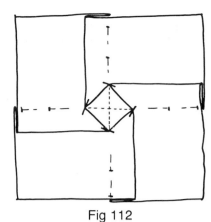

Fig 112

5. Stitch the folds on the outer edges (fig. 113).

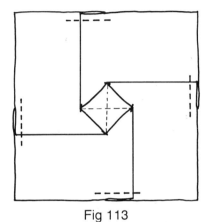

That's it !

Fig 113

This can be done with only one piece of material; but it must be pressed into four, defining the square sections.

Exploring the Possibilities

As the centre is on the bias, the edges will roll. Catch the corners of the central section, through the layers.

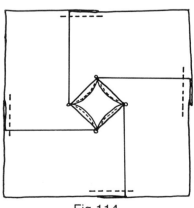

Fig 114

a. Try a small square in this space and roll the folds over to conceal the raw edges. Wadding may be tucked under for a padded effect (fig. 114).

b. Make a miniature Origami Twist and insert in the centre.

c. Embellish with embroidery, quilting, bead work or some pin tucked fabric.

The centre can be altered in size by pinning the original pleats further from the fold - stage 3 in the method.

Further from the fold will increase the size of the central square, nearer the fold will decrease.

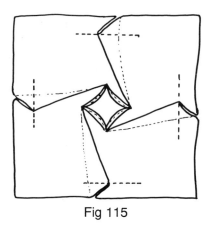

Fig 115

Play with the pleats; these can be twisted, flexed, rolled back or flattened before you secure the outer edge with stitch (fig. 115).

Place the Twist on to wadding/batting, decorate the outer areas with free machine quilting, or top stitch in parallel lines, defining the shapes, or hand or machine quilt any design in the spaces.

Remember that hand quilting will need an additional layer of muslin or fine material, on the back, to catch the quilting.

Look at the back of the work - this can be as interesting as the right side. Here are folds that can be twisted and manipulated into different forms (fig. 116).

Add four triangles to the sides of the Origami patch, turning it on the diagonal.

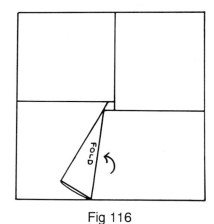

Fig 116

Experiment with different basic shapes. The pleating can be done with a hexagon. This will form a triangle in the centre. Explore the Origami Twist with a rectangle, creating an oblong. Try a triangle!

Some of the other shapes need trimming as the fold does not lie flush with the edge.

The hexagon can be made from three diamonds, or six 60° triangles. Rectangles may be formed from four smaller rectangles.

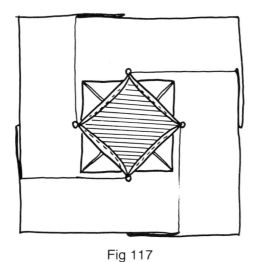

Fig 117

Add Somerset Patches or Prairie Points, tucked under the centre (fig. 117).

Introduce colour -

The basic Twist can be constructed from four differently coloured squares, or from any combination that you wish.

Colour will create more movement, as the Twist will move the colours round; the final result depends on the position of the colours.

Remember that whatever you do -
it will look good.

Extending the "Bow - Tie" !

You may have seen this composition in a textural design called "Bow Tie", which is constructed in the same fashion, but there are many possibilities for playing with the concept.

(There is also a patchwork block of the same name, but made from piecing and not insertion.)

Unlike the Origami Twist, the diagonal central section of the "Bow-Tie" has no seam lines as it is formed from an inserted square and not from a folding technique. As this insertion is on the bias, it has the same properties as the Twist i.e. all the edges roll.

The "Bow-Tie" can be made whatever size you choose and inset into any set of right-angled seams, maybe concealing poor piecing or a mistake or just to add a textured area to the design. It is a very useful trick to have at your finger tips!

There are many resemblances to Cathedral Window Patchwork, in both the construction and the possibilities for embellishment.

It can be expanded, contracted,
rolled over, distorted, twisted -
the list is endless.

Choose either of the following methods to create the Bow-Tie; both have the same result, but one may suit you more than the other.

For both methods, cut 5 squares from the calico, 6" (15cm) is suggested.

Method 1

1. Select your seam allowance.

As the basic shape is a square, the width of seam is irrelevant; the result will either be larger or smaller. Do be consistent!

2. Fold the square and stitch the A/B side. Leave ¼" (.5cm) space at the beginning of the seam (fig. 118).

3. Refold the patch, and sew the B/C side. Leave ¼" (.5cm) space again (fig. 119).

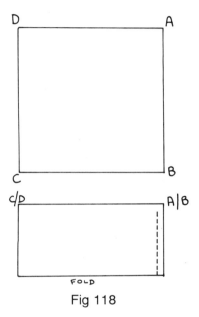

Fig 118

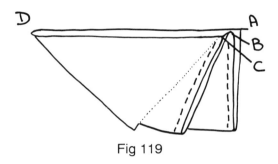

Fig 119

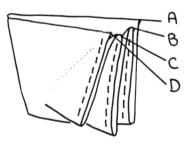

Fig 120

4. Fold again, and sew the C/D side with the same space at the beginning of the seam (fig. 120).

5. Finally fold and stitch the A/D side, remembering to leave the space (fig. 121).

At no point must any of the seams be caught in the stitching; the space has to be left or the shape will not pivot and lie flat.

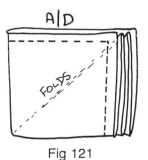

Fig 121

6. Select one of the seams and lay one of the remaining squares on one side and a further one on the other side; effectively you have sandwiched the seam between two squares. Pin the layers together, then sew along the edge with the same selected seam allowance (fig. 122).

Leave the gap!

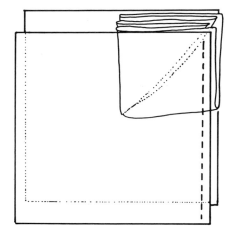
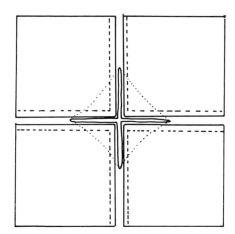

Fig 122

7. Repeat with the next seam, using the adjacent side of one of the attached squares on the back of the seam and adding an additional square to the front; there is another sandwich. Sew again, leaving the space.

8. Continue with the next seam, adding the last spare square. Finally complete the last section, using the adjacent sides of the previously attached squares to form the sandwich; just flex them into place, and complete the seam.

Open out and Bingo!

There is a square on the diagonal, inserted into four seams (fig. 123). Press gently, taking care with the bias edge.

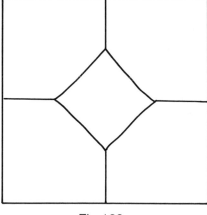

Fig 123

Method 2

1. Fold one of the squares in half, sew down either side (A and B), leaving a ¼" (.5cm) space at the start of the seam (fig. 124).

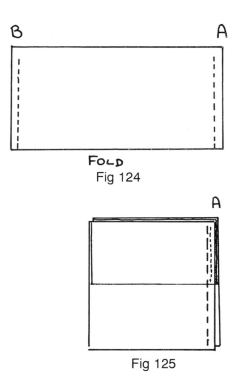

FOLD
Fig 124

2. Select two of the spare squares and sandwich this seam (A) between the edges (fig. 125).

Watch that all the edges are flush with the start of the seam.

3. Repeat on the opposite (B) side (fig. 126).

Fig 125

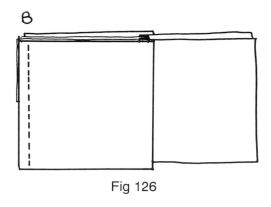

Fig 126

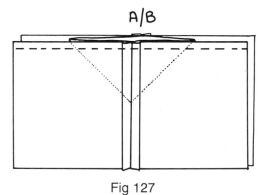

Fig 127

4. Open out and re-fold the shape bringing the sides (A/B) to the centre. Open the seams, pin the pieces together, and stitch across (fig. 127).

Inserting the central section in this manner can cause it to be distorted since aligning all the edges can be awkward. Finger press all the seams open to reduce bulk. An alternative to stitching across would be starting in the centre and stitching outwards.

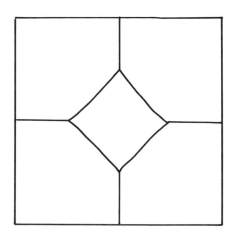

Open out and Bingo again!
A diagonal square inserted into four others.

5. Press gently, being careful with the bias edges.

Developing the Design

Unlike the Origami Twist, the corners of the Bow-Tie do not have to be anchored with a stitch; but this is necessary if you wish to roll the edges. All the ideas given in the previous section on the Origami Twist apply to this design.

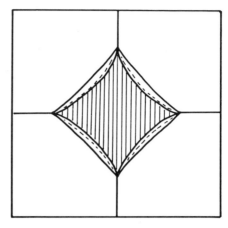

Try the effect of inserting other sized central patches. There is no reason why the central square has to be the identical size as the others; it can be larger or smaller, and will still have the same properties (fig. 128).

Fig 128

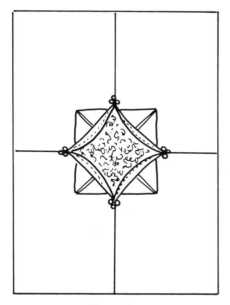

So you can twist, roll, insert a window, decorate the central section, add the Prairie Points or Somerset Patches.The shape need not be inset into squares (fig. 129); it can be set in any set of seams which meet at right angles. This is ideal for concealing an area that has been poorly pieced. (Of course, you designed it specially to fit in there!)

Fig 129

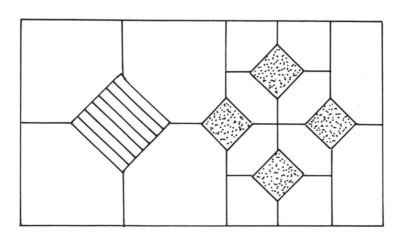

Introduce colours to change the effect. It lends itself to striped materials, as the background sections can be made from stripes travelling in different directions

If the original patch is made in the manner shown in method 1 then turned inside out (the seams will be concealed), it makes an excellent textural appliqué. [See the back of the jacket photograph - page 80.]

Remember to start with the wrong side out if you are using a printed fabric or when you turn it, the result may not be what you wished. Also, leave a slightly larger gap at the start of the sewing otherwise it becomes a trifle difficult to turn through the hole!

Now no one will ever know whether that natty little Textural insert was by choice, or an added extra for a very valid reason. Just a mite more inventive than the ubiquitous Suffolk Puff.

Waistcoats & Jackets

Be individual: construct your own tucked and textured garment using the techniques featured in this book.

The calico jacket in the photographs was made entirely by the "Quilt-as-you-Go" method but two vital ingredients are necessary. One is very expensive and the other uncomfortable!

It was designed the day after returning to England on the "red-eye" flight from Los Angeles, and suffering from the Beijing flu that had decimated L.A. I was determined not to give in to either jet-lag or any old virus. The sewing machine has always been a source of comfort in times of stress and "it seemed like a good idea at the time", but I would not like to repeat the experience in a hurry! Don't look too carefully at the seams, there are some interesting 'designer' wobbles. Of course these little deviations will enhance the individuality of the jacket !!

Now you are reading the book, you will be able to produce your own.

****

80

Creating a Garment

   1. Select a basic pattern.

Jacket and Waistcoat patterns need to be simple, with little tailoring and no darts. Loose fitting sleeves, possibly bat-wing, and bodices are essential; drop shoulders are also advantageous.

Trace the outline on to light-weight vilene; cut out, leaving plenty of excess vilene. Drawing a few straight lines on the vilene will help in positioning the pieces. Pin the vilene to 2oz. wadding (cutting a rough shape larger than the vilene). This forms the base for the textured samples (fig. 130).

Play safe - allow a little extra base materials. Adding the individual sections sometimes causes the base layers to contract.

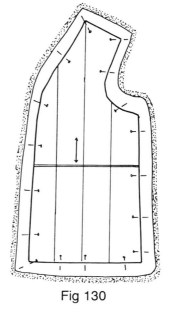

Fig 130

Choose a finer fabric - the garment becomes too bulky otherwise.

   2. Make a variety of textured units; tucked panels and single Bias Tuck bands are possible selections. Pin the central design to the vilene and wadding base, placing parallel to the drawn lines. Baste the panel before adding any further sections. Attach the next pieces with the "Quilt-as-you-Go" method (see section). It is preferable to intersperse heavily textured units with either plain strips or very lightly manipulated bands. Keep the sleeve and underarm panels free from heavily pleated or tucked designs, otherwise you will not be able to move!

Continue building up the design. Allow extra fabric on all the outer lines of the pattern in case there has been some contraction in the sewing (fig. 131).

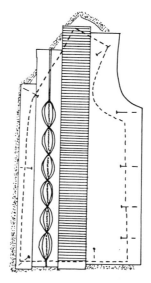

Fig 131

The jacket has a panel of straight tucks down the centre with a single Bias Tuck Band [see page 46]. It also features top-stitching and free machine quilting. The sleeves have a section of Bias Tuck with more quilting and top-stitching; the back includes the Bias Tuck with twisted tucks, Prairie Points and the "Bow-Tie" applied to the shoulder area (fig. 132).

The waistcoat displays Pin Tuck sections and plain tucks, in addition to the Bias Tuck. (See photographs)

Fig 132

3. Once the various panels have been applied, secure all the layers by stitching round the outer edge.

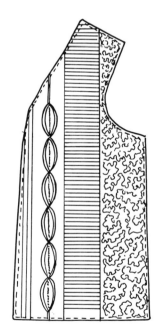

Fig 133

Lay the paper pattern on this worked section, centring the pattern on the relevant section. Pin well. Cut out carefully. Secure all the layers with stitch - some of the previous stitching has been cut through (fig. 133).

4. Using this same technique, construct all the parts of the garment. Following the directions on the instruction sheet, make up the article.

Amaze everyone with your individual creation -
it will be the only one in the World !

Calico Jacket: displaying Tucks, Single Bias Tuck Band and free machine quilting, "Quilt-as-you-go" method (Jennie Rayment).

Drawstring Handbag: with Single Bias Tuck Band embelished with beadwork (Anne Smith).

Cotton Waistcoat: constructed in "Quilt-as-you-go" technique with pin tucks, Single Bias Tuck Band and Tucks in honeycomb design (Shelagh Jarvis).

Confirmation Dress: white silk with pale pink inserts, Bias Tucks and free machine quilting (Lesley Seddon).

Trumpet Cushion: with Somerset Patchwork inserts (Sue Wood).

Silk Cushion: featuring the "Trumpet Voluntary", Origami Twist with ruched piping (Shelagh Jarvis).

Finishing Techniques

This section will cover bordering, quilting, piping, inserting zips into cushion backs, various frilling techniques and making a simple bag.

Having ploughed through all the examples, and created all the samples, a splendid cushion will be absolutely essential on which to rest the weary head, and you will definitely need a bag in which to put everything.

Adding a Border

Many of the samples will need to be framed with fabric to enhance the appearance and neaten the edges; they can then be used for cushions or linked together to make quilts or wall-hangings.

Before you attempt to add any further sections to the work, it is well worth trimming the side edges and cutting them straight. Hopefully, it will not prove too difficult to convert the piece into a geometric shape of some description; a square is the most usual and easiest to adapt for inclusion in the finished cushion, box lid, or part of a quilt.

Now decide on the size of the finished article. First calculate the actual size that you would like to achieve, then add on the seam allowances. It becomes well nigh impossible to make accurate calculations if the seam allowances are included.

1. Measure the sides. Deduct the chosen seam allowance from this figure to calculate the real size after completion.

Do not worry if they are not quite as precise as you had intended; by attaching accurately cut borders, and a little bit of push and pull, they can be corrected.

2. Decide on the ultimate length and breadth of the finished article. Deduct the real size of the textured centre from these measurements; now add the seam allowances to these figures.

Example Sample size = 11½" (29cm) square. Deduct seam allowances [¼" (.5cm)]. Real size = 11" (28cm) square.
Assume desired finished size = 16" (40cm) square.
Therefore subtract 11" from 16" = 5" (12cm). This is the total quantity to be added.
Divide this in half (presuming the article has a border on all sides) equalling 2 ½" (2.5cm).

NOW add on the seam allowances:-
2 ½" + (2 x ¼") = 3" (3.5cm) wide strip.

Having manoeuvred through the complications of mathematics and cut the strip, all you have to do is to stitch it on!

 3. Measure the length of the sides first and cut 2 identical pieces. Place right sides down along opposite edges, pin well, before sewing (fig. 134).

USE AN ACCURATE ¼" (.5cm) SEAM ALLOWANCE.

As the work may well pull out of shape and distort, cutting the strips to a set length and pinning to either end before stitching will keep the distortion under control.

 4. Open out, cut 2 further strips the total length of the remaining sides. Pin as before, then stitch, WITH THE SAME SEAM ALLOWANCE (fig. 135).

Frequently the stitching drifts inwards or outwards as you reach the end of the seam; keep concentrating on the stitching and try not to relax with relief until you have finished.

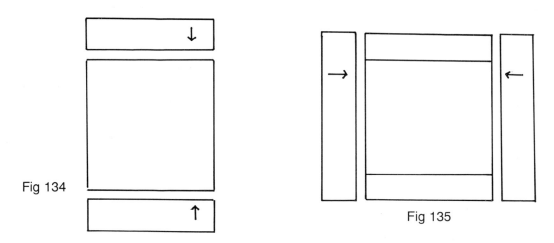

Fig 134

Fig 135

The borders are now in place and the sample can be completed. Stitch several blocks together to make a small textural wall-hanging or a quilt, or turn one into a professional cushion.

Quilting the Work

Many books written on the subject of quilting are readily available from Quilting shops and Libraries for all aficionados of the craft. I have listed several hints and suggestions that you may not have discovered yet.

The preparation for quilting involves placing the work on to wadding/batting, possibly 2oz. or 4oz. polyester, or one of the many other different varieties. In my opinion 2oz. wadding is best for hand quilting. For machine quilted cushions, 4oz. wadding is preferable. Any fabric for a cushion cover can be placed on to 4oz. wadding, even if it is not to be quilted. This prevents the wrinkles from the cushion pad or the filling either showing or coming through the cover. It also enhances the appearance and lengthens the life of the cushion.

Remember - quilting is a way of defining the design, adding texture and anchoring the layers together. Hand quilting always requires a backing fabric, but machine quilting does not.

With hand quilting, the stitch will not be so well defined unless there is a backing material to catch the stitch; also wadding alone is not firm enough to retain the fine stitching. But machine sewing holds so firmly that backing is not required.

Should the feed dogs catch when you are machine quilting, ordinary paper or tissue paper can be placed underneath; this will either fall off or can be torn away afterwards.

Relax about the hand quilting. There is such a lot of "hype" talked about stitch length, quantity of stitches to the inch, etc. For instance, the Japanese style of quilting - Sashiko - displays much larger stitches with a thick gauge thread. Different hands work in different ways and everyone's flexibility varies; you may not be able to manipulate the needle in the same manner - that's your story! In addition, there is no doubt that fine, well-washed fabrics quilt more easily than un-washed firm weaves.

Now, I have given you several valid excuses for the quality of your hand-quilting; the only rule is -

Keep the stitch lengths and spaces in between as even as possible.

Don't forget to sew on the outer edges to anchor the layers together before you complete the article.

As previously mentioned, unlike hand quilting machine quilting does not need a backing fabric. Should you use a backing material, there is a chance that it will ruck up and distort on the back, unless you have tacked the layers and have a walking foot or use the free-hand darning foot. Most machines will quilt adequately through 4oz. wadding/batting although Elna sewing machines appear to function better with paper on the back as the feed dog teeth catch in the wadding.

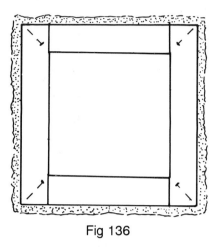

Fig 136

To prepare for any machine quilting, cut a piece of 4oz. wadding and gently press the work on to it. Pin the layers together on the corners, placing the pins pointing outwards (fig. 136).

Machine Quilting

There are several ways to machine quilt; three of them are -

1. "Stitch in the Ditch"

This is quilting along the join (ditch) between the seams, the idea being to stay in the ditch and not deviate!

To quilt a multi-coloured sample, match the thread to one of the colours and attempt to limit any meanders on to this fabric. (Use of invisible thread does disguise the mistakes.) Placing your hands gently on either side of the seam and keeping it flat enables you to see the join more easily. Maintain a moderate even speed although some sewing machines cannot be operated this way; it's all or nothing. (This makes it very difficult to control!) Set a longer stitch length as the wadding causes the stitch to contract. When turning a corner, lower the needle into the seam, raise the presser foot and pivot round. Some presser feet are very hard to align as the size of the foot obscures the seam. Finally I have discovered that wearing bi-focals does make it awkward to see the seam line - a good excuse!!

2. Top Stitching or Echo Quilting

Using the edge of the presser foot as a guide, follow round the outlines of the shape you wish to delineate (fig. 137). Again use a longer stitch length, drop the needle into the work on corners and pivot round on.

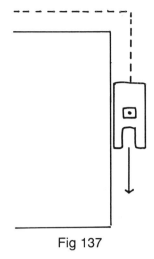

Thread choice can add a further dimension to the appearance. But if you are not too confident, use   matching threads to the fabric and the deviations from the chosen path will be less obvious.

Fig 137

3. Free Machine Quilting

There is no doubt that practice makes perfect; well, it improves it. This is one of those techniques that needs a relaxed operator (glass of wine recommended before commencing). Push the sewing machine further away than normal. Sit comfortably; lean towards the machine keeping the spine straight, pushing the bottom out and rest your elbows on the table to take the weight. The wrists need to be free and flexible. Relax and drop your shoulders; students with rigid shoulders under their ears do not perform so well.

So you are sitting correctly, have consumed the vino and have relaxed. You have lowered the feed dogs, inserted the darning foot, positioned the work under the needle and all you have to do is construct a series of rounded squiggles. These should not cross over each other nor have points or spikes but flow evenly over the selected area (fig. 138).

Bet the telephone rings!

Try it; grasp the material firmly, do not have flat hands. Bring the lower thread to the top surface to prevent it tangling underneath. Maintain an even speed as you swing the work in a series of arcs (similar to steering a car). Relax!

Fig 138

Some sewing machines do not have a darning foot but there may be a lever or knob that controls the amount of pressure on the presser foot (see instruction book). By reducing the pressure to zero and using the ordinary presser foot, it is possible to free machine quilt although not so easy.

Use of this technique will add further texture to the surface of the design. It is difficult at first but keep experimenting and if you cannot achieve the random curves - have spikes!

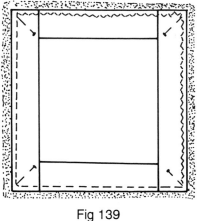

Fig 139

Once the sample has been quilted, sew round the edge to secure all the layers; a long stitch length or wide zig-zag is ideal (fig. 139). It is not possible to add piping or frills if the outer edge is not stabilised.

Decorative Edging
Techniques

Piping

Piping is easy if you use this method, and will add a further texture to the work. Once again, there are many opposing views on the construction, and the technique suggested may be contrary to other well- established ways.

In this technique, the fabric strips to cover the cord are cut across the material; there is no reason to cut on the bias. (Making the tube of continuous bias is complicated; it is rarely as straight as strips cut with the rotary cutter and has seams in a variety of places.)

The strips for piping with the straight grain of the material MUST be cut across the fabric, i.e. selvedge to selvedge. It will not work otherwise.

For all cotton, chintz and calico type materials, this is the best way, but if you are working with thick weaves or velvet or non-cotton fabrics, a bias-cut strip is better. In addition, when using striped patterns a bias cut is more effective.

For cutting strips on the bias see Chapter on the Bias Tuck.

How to Pipe

1. Measure the length or circumference of the piece. Cut sufficient 1½" (4cm) wide strips, if necessary join together with a straight seam, trim any excess and open the seam out, and press flat.

2. Cut the same measurement of No. 4 piping cord.

Should you buy the inexpensive cord, it does have to be washed to prevent shrinkage; the better quality cords need not be washed if you follow this method. Who ever remembers to boil the cord?

Working by hand follow the same instructions as for the machine.

3. Put the zipper foot on the machine setting the needle on your left, i.e. away from the body of the machine.

Bernina users, remember to move the needle position over!

Set a long stitch length for speed. Lay the cord on the wrong side of the strip, setting down by 1½" (4 cm). Fold the fabric over, lining up the edges (fig. 140).

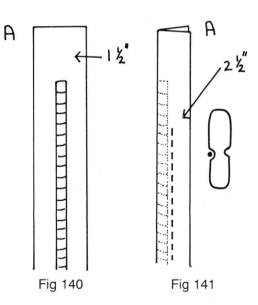

Fig 140   Fig 141

4. Commence sewing 1" (2.5cm) below the start of the cord. Place the finger of your left hand alongside the cord and hold the edges of the fabric together with the right hand; there is no necessity to pin. Sew to the end (fig. 141).

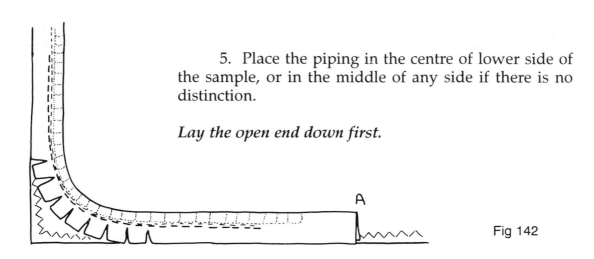

5. Place the piping in the centre of lower side of the sample, or in the middle of any side if there is no distinction.

Lay the open end down first.

A

Fig 142

6. Sew clockwise round the work, matching the edges of the piping to the edges of the sample. Stop approximately 3" (7cm) from any corner, clip well and curve the cord in a gentle arc (fig. 142).

Too sharp a curve will result in a pointed corner to the finished article. Please do not pin the piping as a better result will occur if the piping can flex by itself; one tends to sew to the pins rather than allowing the cord to float round.

7. If piping round a shape, continue until you approach the start of the cord; stop 3" (7cm) away. Fold over the raw edge - A - ¼" (.5cm). Open, trim the other end of the piping, butting it up exactly to the beginning.

Fold the excess fabric over this join and sew past (fig. 143).

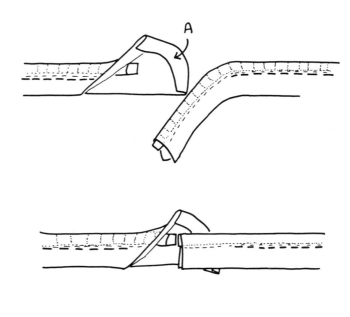

As the ends of the cord are butted together and hidden in two layers of fabric, this junction will conceal any shrinkage in the cord when washed. (You can tell if your friends have washed their cushions by gently feeling this junction and see if there is a gap!!)

Fig 143

Ruched Piping

For an enhanced textural effect make ruched piping instead. It requires a wider strip than the previous method.

1. Cut 2″ (5cm) strips (3 x the circumference). Join all the pieces together, pressing open the seams and trimming off any excess.

2. Cut a length of cord the exact measurement of the sample. Pin the end of the cord firmly to the start of the strip, setting down by 1½″ (4cm). Place the normal straight stitch presser foot on the machine. Fold the fabric over, matching the edges, and sew, keeping edge of the presser foot along the piping cord (fig. 144).

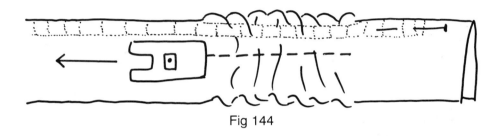

Fig 144

This will make a channel, and when you reach the end of the cord, it can be pulled up; the fabric will ruche on to the cord.

3. Continue until the end, then pin the cord to the strip to prevent it un-gathering. Spread the gathers evenly along the cord.

This is applied in the same manner as the previous method, although there is no need to clip on the corner curves. It is very difficult to complete the final butting of the cords and requires a little persuasion; but the finished effect is delightful.

Watch that the cord round the corners does not become too tight - ease gently.

Frilling Techniques

Frills can be gathered, pleated, ruched or contain piping. The frill may be as full as you like, but if the gathered effect is desired, it will appear more luxurious if there is plenty of material.

There's nothing like a good frill - to enhance your work!

Gathered Frills

Measure the circumference, or length of side to contain the frill, and multiply this figure by either 2 or 3 (three times the length will be more ornate). Decide on the depth of frill required, then cut strips of fabric twice this measurement, not omitting to add the seam allowance of ½" (1.5cm) to either side.

Remember to cut across the fabric - selvedge to selvedge.

1. Join all the lengths together, trimming seams and pressing open. Join the ends together, forming a circle.

Check there is no twist in the circle.

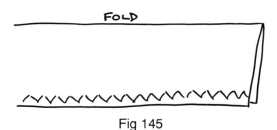

Fig 145

2. Fold in half, press well. Stitch along the lower edge to prevent movement when gathering (fig. 145).

3. Gathering can be done in a variety of ways. Before starting, mark the length of the frill in four equal stages - use a pin or light pencil mark.

a. By hand - gather up the four sections to fit the desired space.

b. Use a long stitch on the sewing machine - gather the four sections individually (there is less chance of the thread snapping).

c. Use a Ruffler - this is a special gadget that is attached to the machine and will ruffle the fabric. It is an optional extra for the machine although some older models will have them in the attachments box; it resembles an instrument of Mediaeval torture! I admit this will ruffle beautifully, but the ultimate measurement of the frill is pure guesswork, as the instructions are unfathomable, and omit to take account of the thickness of the fabric, size of stitch-length etc. So it is by guess and by God, but it pulls out easily and you can always do it again.

This is not the same as the gathering foot that some machines have. These will gather fine fabrics and lace but not always anything thick.

d. Use the cord method - this is ideal for any machine.

Cut a length of cord, the circumference of the work plus 2″ (5cm) - 3″ (8cm). Use button hole thread, fine strong crotchet thread, stranded embroidery silk or similar.

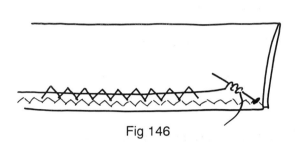

Fig 146

Pin the start of the cord on to the edge of the frill and set the machine for a wide zig-zag, the widest and longest it will do. Sew over the cord; by pulling it up above the foot and through the slit, you are less likely to stitch through (fig. 146).

When you reach the end of the cord, raise the presser foot and pull more cord through. This will start to gather up the material as it goes.

This is the same situation as pushing the wire through the heading of a net curtain; the wire is the correct length and the curtain will ruche on to the wire.

Tie the loose ends together; as the cord was the correct length, the frill will fit the work.

4. Pin the frill to the work, lining all the edges. Stitch, using the zipper foot, ensuring that plenty of frill is in the corners, or it will appear tight (fig. 147).

Do not panic if the frill does not go hard up to the piping; all the excessive stitching now showing will be concealed when the back is applied.

It is not always necessary to pipe but you may find it easier when adding a frill, as the ridge of the piping provides a guideline to sew round.

Fig 147

****

Ruched Frill

See the Ruching Chapter (page 28)

Measure the circumference or the length of the article to be frilled. Make the frill the same dimensions as described in the Frill section.

Remember to divide the fabric into four equal parts, then gather either side of the strip, independently. Adjust the quantity of frill so it will fit the sides. Fold over and anchor the edges together before applying as in the previous section.

If the initial strips are cut on the bias, the frill will have a more rounded appearance, as opposed to a crisper, more ridged effect if the strips are cut on the straight grain.

Piped Frill

This was discovered by accident. I am not sure whether it is a set formula or not. The piping cord is enclosed in this frill and the frill drawn up on it. This is a combination of ruched piping and a frill; it saves fabric and a bit of time, and it is different.

1. Decide on the overall depth of the frill (see page 92) and allow 1" (2.5cm) seam allowance to both edges. Cut the strips with the rotary cutter and join together into the circle, trimming and pressing the seams open. Put the normal straight stitch foot on the machine.

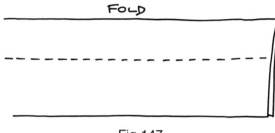

Fig 147

2. Cut the cord the exact length of the side or circumference of the work. Sew along the frill 1" (2.5cm) from the edge. Open out, and lay in the cord. Pin the end to the fabric (fig. 148).

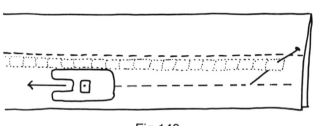

Fig 148

3. Leaving the normal presser foot in place, sew along the cord as in Ruched Piping, gathering up when you reach the end of the cord. Continue until you approach the first end and pin the other end of the cord to the fabric.

Shuffle the gathers evenly along the cord. It is now ready to apply (fig. 149).

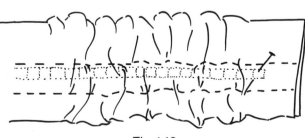

Fig 149

Watch the butting up of the cords' junction; it is a little awkward, but with a modicum of patience, you will succeed.

Finally, after all this extra labour, the back can be applied.

Who said piping and frilling was easy?

Backing the Work

Wall-hangings, mats, small quilts, tie-backs etc. will not need a zip inserted, but you may like to put a zip in the back of a cushion. There are other ways of closing a cushion and at the risk of total annihilation in public, I feel that it is preferable either to have a zip, or not to bother at all, simply closing the cushion (after the pad has been inserted) by stitching up. The pillowcase method is not a favourite of mine.

The choice is yours!

Should you decide not to have a zipped back, please omit the next section. I will not tempt you with a simple method.

Inserting a Zip

This can all be done by hand. Back stitch in the same places as indicated for the machine.

When purchasing a zip, it is not important for it to measure the full width of the article; a 12″ (30cm) zip will take 16″ (40cm) - 18″ (45cm) cushion pads. Plastic teeth zips can be any length as they can be trimmed to suit.

1. Measure the overall width and length of the article. Cut a rectangle of fabric that is 1″ - 1½″ (3-4cm) longer than the item; keep the same width.

Cut out with the longer length down the grain, i.e. selvedge parallel to increased length.

2. Fold up 4″ (10cm) on the longer sides, right sides together, and press fold. Lay zip on fold and with a pencil mark the beginning and end of the teeth, or approximately 1½″ (4cm) from outer edge (fig. 150).

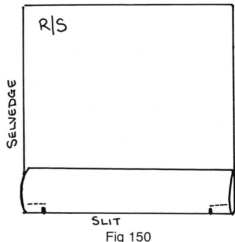

Fig 150

Fig 151

3. Sew in from outer edge to this mark using ½" (1.5cm) seam allowance. Sew forward and reverse for a firm seam. See Fig. 150.

4. Slit this edge and press open seams (fig. 151).

Should there not be enough material to have a whole piece as the back is slit, there is no reason why two sections cannot be joined in this manner.

5. Lay the zip in the opening, with the head positioned as in the diagram.

Remember to have the zip placed face down - it is very hard to open otherwise!

Fasten the zip head end to the seam with a pin on either side (fig. 152).

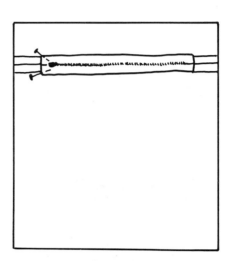

Fig 152

6. Put the zipper foot on the machine; the foot is now on the left of the needle, i.e. needle on the inside. Turn the material over, right side facing. Open the zip 2" (5cm) and commence sewing with a small seam, approximately ¼" (.5cm). Drop the needle into the work when the zip head is reached, raise the presser foot, slide the zip head past. Continue sewing until the end of the zip, lining up fold with mid-point of zip teeth, turn and sew across the end (fig. 153).

Watch the needle if the teeth are metal!

Fig 153

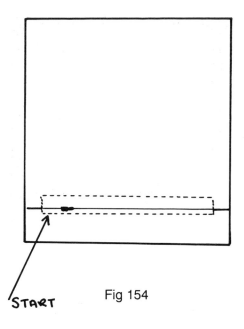

START Fig 154

7. Take a slightly larger seam on the return journey, lapping the fold fractionally over the lower fold.

This overlap will prevent the teeth showing when the pad is inserted.

Drop the needle into the work approximately 2" (5cm) from end, slide the zip head past and continue to the end; turn and complete the seam (fig. 154). Finish off by pulling threads through to the back, tie together and either trim or weave ends into fabric seam with a needle.

Congratulate yourself! Open the zip a few inches or it will be awkward to move when you have applied the back.

****

Applying the Back to the Masterpiece!

1. Pin the back to the front, positioning the zip at the bottom (fig. 155). Move needle to the left side of presser foot. Sew round twice, setting the needle and foot outside the cord, then push hard up to the piping (fig. 156).

DO NOT STITCH INSIDE THE CORD OR IT WILL DISAPPEAR WHEN YOU TURN THE WORK RIGHT SIDE OUT!!!

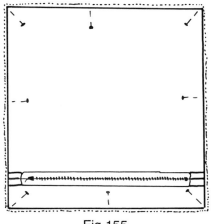

Fig 155

Push really hard with the left hand fingertips, trying to get the needle close to the cord. The arm may well ache with the strain.

Bernina users cannot do this as the needle fits inside the presser foot. You can push until you are blue in the face and it will not succeed. But purchase of a Piping Foot will solve this problem; the groove in the presser foot will sit on the cord allowing the needle to travel next to the piping.

Fig 156

2. Turn to the right side and check that all the stitching is now hidden; if not, sew again and push a little harder especially on the corners. TRY not to stitch over the cord or it will vanish!

Clip and trim any excess material. Push a pad in and

ADMIRE!

Buying a Pad

Many different types of cushion pads are available, ranging from feather to man-made fibres such as polyester. Select which is the most suitable for your requirements.

Pads should always be 1" (2.5cm) larger than the finished item, or the same size as the incomplete article before you pipe it.

Making a Simple Bag

This is the fastest and quickest lined bag with handles that I have ever made. It is so easy, and the principle can be adapted for constructing any size of bag.

"Oh yes", we have all heard that before, but I promise you all that this is the first bag from Lesson 1 in a beginner's class, and there are a huge number around. I can spot a student a mile away still using the bag!

It requires four pieces of material exactly the same size, viz. two outside ones which could be textured samples, plus two pieces of lining material - calico is admirable. Quilt the outside sections on to 4oz. wadding (not forgetting to sew the outer edges to the wadding). In addition, make two handles - see chapter on Weaving with Fabric. Turn the raw edge under when you construct the handles; do ensure they are of equal length.

Fig 157

1. Lay one handle on the top of one outside piece and stitch firmly, back and forwards within the seam allowance.

Handles should be 5" (13cm) - 6" (15cm) apart or wherever you choose - any length from 14" (35cm) for short handles to infinity if you like!

Repeat this operation with the other handle and outside section (fig. 157).

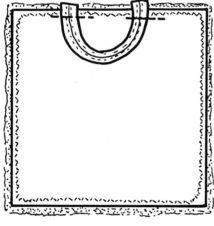

Fig 158

2. Lay the lining on this edge and stitch using a good ¼" (1cm) seam allowance (fig. 158). Repeat with the other half.

3. Open out these oblongs (rectangles). Lay right sides together and pin, matching the seams. Commence sewing from the centre seam (fig. 159). Curve round the corners and sew to the end of the lining.

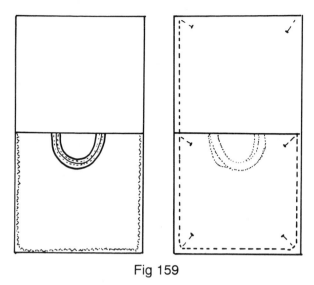

Fig 159

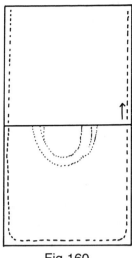

Fig 160

4. Flip over and complete the last seam. Trim any excess (fig. 160).

This ensures the outside sections match easily.

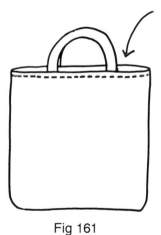

Fig 161

5. Turn right side through the gap before stitching up and push the lining into the bag, poking the corners out. Finally, to retain the lining within the bag, top stitch round the edge, taking care over the thick side seams (fig. 161).

Well, was I right ?

Glossary

Backing: The fabric used underneath a sample or the underside of a cushion or quilt.

Baste: Securing of layers with a long stitch to prevent movement.

Batting: Wadding or filling frequently made from polyester fibres used in-between or underneath fabric for quilting purposes.

Bias: Diagonal of the woven grain (45 degrees to the selvedge).

Borders: Fabric attached to the outer edges to frame the sample.

Box Pleats: Pairs of pleats folded towards each other.

Calico: Plain woven strong cotton cloth (sometimes bleached) with a distinctive fleck in the weave. (British definition.)

Cathedral Window Patchwork: Traditional design contructed from folded and stitched squares.

Chintz: Close-weave shiny cotton cloth with a resin coating that gives it the characteristic sheen.

Crettonne: A washable hard-wearing fabric similar to unglazed chintz; liable to shrink.

Crimplene: Stretchy material produced from man-made fibres.

Gabardine: A lightweight closely woven fabric with a prominent diagonal rib.

Grain: Direction of the weave. Weft fibres run across from selvedge to selvedge. Warp fibres are parallel to the selvedge.

Log Cabin/Pineapple Patchwork: Traditional designs made from strips of material.

Mercerised Cotton: Treated to look like silk.

Muslin: Fine soft cotton fabric resembling gauze in appearance. (British definition.)

Pin Tucks: Fine tucks sometimes enclosing a cord.

Ruche/Ruching: Gathered material often in a strip, used for decorative effect.

Satin Stitch: The zig-zag effect produced by increasing the stitch width and decreasing the stitch length on the sewing machine.

Seam Allowance: Distance between the stitch line and the edge of the fabric.

Selvedge/selvage: The firm edges of the fabric running parallel to the warp threads.

Somerset/Folded Patchwork: Design made with folded squares of fabric, worked from the centre outwards on lines relating to equal points of the compass.

Space Dyed Threads: Fibres dyed in a variety of separate colours.

Suffolk Puff: Gathered circle of fabric sometimes stuffed with wadding or containing an inserted circle of contrasting material. Widely used in Victorian times.

Vanishing Pen: Pen containing special chemical ink that disappears in time.

Vilene: Interfacing developed from bonded fibres.

Wadding: Batting or filling frequently made from polyester fibres used in-between or underneath fabric for quilting purposes.

Warp: Threads stretched lengthwise on the loom.

Weft: Threads woven into and crossing the warp.

List of Suppliers

The Cotton Patch
1285 Stratford Road
Hall Green
Birmingham B28 9AJ
Tel: 0121 702 2840
Fax: 0121 778 5924

Country Crafts
10a St. Mary's Walk
Hailsham, East Sussex
Tel: 01323 442271

Country Threads
2 Pierrepoint Place
Bath BA1 1JX
Tel: 01225 480056

Creative Quilting
3 Bridge Road
Hampton Court
Surrey KT8 9EU
Tel: 0181 941 7075

Faberdashery
8a Midhurst Walk
West Street, Midhurst
West Sussex GU29 9NF
Tel: 01730 817889

Green Hill
27 Bell Street
Romsey
Hampshire SO51 8GY
Tel: 01794 517973

Patchworkers Paradise
16 East Street
Blandford Forum
Dorset DT11 7DR
Tel: 01258 456099

Patchwork Plus
129 Station Road
Cark-in-Cartmel
Grange-over-Sands
Cumbria LA11 7NY
Tel: 015395 59009

Purely Patchwork
23 High Street
Linlithgow
Scotland EH49 7AB
Tel/Fax: 01506 846200

Quilters Cottage
60 Bridge Street
Garstang, Preston
Lancs PR3 1YB
Tel: 01995 603929

Quilters Haven
Rendlesham Mews
Rendlesham
Woodbridge, Suffolk
Tel: 01394 461183

The Quilt Room
20 West Street
Dorking
Surrey RH4 1BL
Tel: 01306 740739
Fax: 01306 877407

Village Fabrics
Unit 7a
Bushells Business Estate
Hithercroft
Wallingford
Oxon OX10 9DD
Tel: 01491 836178
Fax: 01491 825565

You Toucan Quilt
Windsor House
Greville Road
Bedminster
Bristol BS3 1LL
0117 9632599

Bibliography

Conran, Terence. The Soft Furnishings Book. Book Club Associates, 1986.

Fishburn, Angela. Curtains and Window Treatments. B.T. Batsford Ltd, 1982.

Frutiger, Adrian. Signs and Symbols. Studio Editions, 1991.

Halsey, Mike & Youngmark, Lore. Foundations of Weaving.
David & Charles, 1986.

Jackson, Paul. The Encylopedia of Origami and Papercraft Techniques.
Headline Book Publishing, 1991.

Poster, Donna. The Quilter's Guide to Rotary Cutting. Chiltern Book
Company, 1991.

Workshops and Lectures

Contact Jennie Rayment for the list of workshops, demonstrations and lectures.

Wren Cottage, 3 The Millstream, Haslemere,
Surrey. GU27 3QA. Tel: 01428 652495

More Tucks and Textures

There is a following publication called **Tucks and Textures Two** which will be available in December 1996 containing further innovative and exciting ideas with texture, microwave dyeing and various projects to make. These will include – the Pilgrims Scrip Handbag (similar to Drawstring Handbag – photograph opposite page 82) and the Woven Handbag featured on the front cover in addition to several other creations. To obtain a copy please contact:-

J. R. Publications – Wren Cottage, 3 The Millstream, Haslemere, Surrey GU27 3QA. Tel: 01428 652495.
